D0953454

Somebody Is Going to Die if Lilly Beth Doesn't Catch That Bouquet

Somebody Is Going to Die if Lilly Beth Doesn't Catch That Bouquet

THE OFFICIAL SOUTHERN LADIES'
GUIDE TO HOSTING THE
PERFECT WEDDING

Gayden Metcalfe
and
Charlotte Hays

 HYPERION

NEW YORK

Library of Congress Cataloging-in-Publication Data

Metcalfe, Gayden.
    Somebody is going to die if Lily Beth doesn't catch that bouquet : the official southern
ladies' guide to hosting the perfect wedding / Gayden Metcalfe and Charlotte Hayes.—1st ed.
        p. cm.
    ISBN-13: 978-1-4013-0295-5
    ISBN 1-4013-0295-5
    1. Weddings—Southern States—Planning. 2. Wedding etiquette. I. Hays, Charlotte. II.
Title.
    HQ745.M635 2007
    395.2'2—dc22   2006046903

Hyperion books are available for special promotions and premiums.
For details contact Michael Rentas, Assistant Director, Inventory
Operations, Hyperion, 77 West 66th Street, 11th floor,
New York, New York 10023, or call 212-456-0133.

Design by Jo Anne Metsch

FIRST EDITION

10 9 8 7 6 5 4 3 2 1

FOR
JULIA LIPSCOMB GOODRICH
HARLEY METCALFE III

Contents

Contents

TOP TEN DELTA
WEDDING RECEPTION FOODS

Wedding Cake

Punch

Champagne

Open Bar

Cheese Straws

Mints

Salted Nuts

Finger Sandwiches
(at least one with chicken salad)

Tartlets with assorted fillings

An Arrangement of white grapes,
strawberries, and cheese on a silver tray

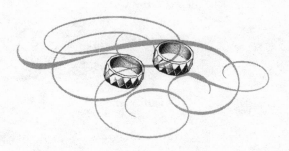

TOP TEN FOODS *NOT* TO SERVE AT YOUR WEDDING RECEPTION

Cold Duck "Champagne"

Drummets

Hot Wings

Chips and Dips

Cocktail Weenies

Cold Cuts

*Processed Cheese Cubes
with Toothpicks*

*Anything on a Saltine
or Ritz Cracker*

Rib Tips

Trash

Somebody Is Going to Die if Lilly Beth Doesn't Catch That Bouquet

1

There Will Always Be One
More Last Delta Wedding

I N THE MISSISSIPPI DELTA, funerals bring out the best in people, while weddings, which are supposed to be happy occasions, bring out the worst. It takes a strong love to survive a Delta wedding. Funerals bring out our genuineness; weddings bring out our pretentiousness. A lady we know is still smarting from the time, several years ago, she was asked in to view a relative's wedding presents. "I'm glad you could come now," said Cousin Snooty, mother of the bride, "because I won't have room for you at the wedding." Actually, this was unusual in the Delta, because we tend to invite everybody we know, plus some. But at least Cousin Snooty made sure everybody had an opportunity to see the gifts (and certainly to give one).

A carpenter had been called in to build a tiered, bleacher-like affair that was draped in white organdy, with bows and swags. The custom of displaying wedding presents in this manner has gone down as the price of silver has gone up. Brides now in their forties are probably the last generation to have observed this tradition.

A Delta wedding is an extravaganza that has been years in the making (for the exception to this rule, please see, "weddings, shotgun," page 155). Weddings in the Delta do not begin with a young man's proposal of holy matrimony—they begin the moment a squirming bride-to-be is presented in swaddling clothes to her mother's arms at the King's Daughters Hospital in Greenville, Mississippi, where the nicer Delta babies are born. A small but choice group, it must be noted, composed of several of the very nicest of Greenville babies, was born in Greenwood, a town with which in ordinary circumstances we are highly competitive. But several Greenville matrons admired a prominent physician so much that, when he took his practice to Greenwood, instead of begging their husbands to shoot him, they followed him. Driving fifty miles to go to the doctor or a party is nothing in the Delta. Because of this distance, however, one baby was almost born on her father's airplane in the doctor's front yard—her mother had waited until the last minute. Being told by his wife that a plane was landing in his yard, Dr. Poindexter reportedly replied, "Adelaide, I told you not to have that last scotch and water."

Peering into her baby's eyes, whether in Greenwood or the King's Daughters, the Delta mother beholds the future: cheerleading, Chi Omega, and that special day when her beautiful daughter will waft up the aisle on the arm of her father (if she is a genuine Delta bride, you will smell her before you actually see her—we are a people of the perfume bottle, and other bottles, too). The Delta wedding is the apotheosis of all the mother's dreams—and, of course, all her social ambitions. A father, whose role, as one local matron put it, is to sit up, to pay up, and to shush up, is expected to behave like a good child: seen but not heard.

Another important extra is a groom. In the Delta, you still can't have a wedding without one. His job is to be presentable at all times and exude ecstasy because a paragon of Southern womanhood has done him the honor of accepting his offer of holy matrimony, even if being united in that blessed state requires a production that would have put Mr. Cecil B. DeMille of Hollywood in Whitfield. (Whitfield is our state mental institution. We affectionately refer to it as "the bin," which is nicer than loony bin.) After being in one of our weddings, you'll feel you've been to the bin, or ought to head there immediately. We have a special name for a Delta wedding that is an unusually elaborate, or famous, or perhaps notorious, or, in some undefined way, a particularly noteworthy occasion—for some reason, which none of us now remember, we always call it "the last Delta wedding." Any wedding of epic proportions is accorded the high accolade of being designated a last Delta wedding; there have been hundreds upon hundreds of last Delta weddings over the years. As long as there is a Delta, there will be one more last Delta wedding.

Before we leave the King's Daughters, there is one more consideration regarding the initial stages of wedding planning: The Southern mother wants her daughter to have a proud old Southern name that conjures up the notion of fine breeding. To this end, we like names redolent of our Virginia or Kentucky pasts, real or imagined. This has created a Delta-wide penchant for last names as first names for girls. For this reason, the Mississippi Delta has the lowest Janet-quotient of any region in the United States. Suitable names for a Delta girl are Dabney, Meriwether, Harper, and Bland (didn't they have a county in Virginia?), though in day-to-day parlance, the bearers of these fine old Southern names will likely go by Baby Doll, Presh (which is actually short for Precious), or Sistuh.

By the time a Delta girl is eight years old, she knows more about wedding etiquette than a Yankee bridal consultant. By the time she is ten, she has given serious thought to selecting a silver pattern—preferably Rich Aunt Bess's, to facilitate inheritance. We like to say we are born this way, that we Delta girls inherit an etiquette gene. In reality, it's a mixture of nature and nurture. We were toddling up aisles in flower girl outfits in real weddings or participating in Tom Thumb weddings at St. James' Episcopal Church, an especially nice place to get married, as soon as we could put one foot in front of the other. Still, very young children sometimes make a faux pas, even in the Delta. When Dexter and Davenport, the Jenkins twins, were ring bearer and flower girl respectively in a big wedding in Hollandale, Mississippi, they got up the aisle just fine. Then they plopped unceremoniously down on the steps leading to the sanctuary. When the door opened to admit the bride, a fire truck with sirens blaring passed by; hearing this clarion call, the children fled and had chased the fire truck halfway down the block before somebody caught them and brought them back to church.

We are also particular about what the children wear. One of the most important rules: Do not dress your ring bearer up like a miniature man. This rule cannot be sufficiently stressed. There is nothing cute about a four-year-old boy in a tiny suit or a tux. The proper ring bearer wears an Eton suit, which has short pants and a circular collar—we may pronounce it E-ton, and while some of us don't know that the name comes from a school in England that is even older than Ole Miss, we know that little boys look sweet in an E-ton suit. We're still talking bad about the tacky bride whose ring bearer wore itty-bitty tails, with a white tie, just like the grown-ups. Even in the Delta, there are people who Don't Know.

Alice Hunt McAllister, who lives in New York City, shudders every time she tells her sad story about a little boy who tried to sit by her in church. When Alice Hunt realized that he was wearing a clip-on bowtie and long pants, she moved to another pew quicker than if he'd had cholera. "I didn't want a homunculus sitting in my lap," she harrumphed. A homunculus is what alchemists called a teeny-tiny little man that hasn't been born yet, and they are ugly as sin.

The Southern girl knows before she is accepted into the Dirt Daubers Garden Club that it is wrong to bring a wedding present to the reception (it has been sent previously—you have one year to write a thank-you note, but the Southern bride will write a gushing note almost before you get home from mailing the gift). While still in her high chair, the Southern girl has heard her mother utter an all-important dictum. "Reply in kind." That means that a formal invitation requires a formal reply (in black ink—and *not* ink from a ballpoint pen) in the same form as the invitation: "Miss Dabney Harper Jones accepts the kind invitation of . . ." Dabney Harper Jones will reply like this if the invitation is from her cousin next door. A less formal invitation calls for a less formal reply. Hence Mama's reply-in-kind rubric. The Southern girl at a very early age is conversant with the proper role of the usher: The mother takes the usher's arm, while her husband and children follow her up the aisle. The late Margaret Reynolds, a revered member of our community whose job it was to prepare the wedding party, laid down a rule for ushers during the rehearsal: "Keep your sword arm free," Mrs. Reynolds always ordered. She was oblivious to the effect this injunction had on visitors from the North, whose eyes always bulged with fear, but it is a good mnemonic device to prevent an usher from offering a lady the wrong arm. The sword arm, the right one, is kept free for the exclusive use of the young lady, to whom it is presented on the way up and down the aisle.

Alice Hunt McAllister, who seems to do nothing but run into pitiful etiquette mishaps up north, also had a very unfortunate experience with regard to proper ushering. This time she was attending a wedding in Washington, D.C. It seems that Alice Hunt took the usher's arm, expecting to sail up the aisle. Halfway up, she realized she was dragging the poor man. "That poor little leprechaun left skid marks on the floor," Alice Hunt has recalled many, many times. Alice Hunt seriously considered throwing the book—the Amy Vanderbilt book, which otherwise was hidden at the bottom of her closet for emergency consultation only—at somebody. (It is okay to peek at an etiquette book, but if you rely too heavily on it, people will think that you are not fully acquainted with what is right and wrong and could fall into the unattractive category of People Who Don't Know.)

We expect Southern girls to have digested all these etiquette rules and to go out of their way to behave, at weddings and elsewhere. Southern mothers have a dictum: "Even if it kills you, be nice." If you e'vuh do anything bad, the mother always adds, somebody who knows your parents, or your grandparents, will be present and we will hear about it. That is why it is never safe to be rude in the Mississippi Delta. There are no secrets here, which is fun unless you're the one provoking the juicy gossip.

Southerners have been told from infancy that they must always go around the room and speak to the older ladies and gentlemen at any party. "Did you speak to the chaperones?" Olivia Morgan Gilliam once asked a daughter who was hugging the commode for dear life and barely able to speak to Olivia Morgan at that point. We will speak to the older ladies and gentlemen even if we are so blind drunk that we barely know our own names, much less theirs. It's considered all right to get drunk as long as it doesn't impede doing the right thing. For example, we know one Memphis father of whom it was said that, no matter how drunk his daughters got Saturday night, he always made sure to get them up and go to Second Presbyterian Sunday morning. One of the most courtly Southern gentlemen we know is Bo Crittenden, who just happens to be a direct descendent of a famous general in The War (by which we mean the late unpleasantness with our friends to the north), who was always so inebriated that an aide de camp had to tell him whether they had won or lost the battle.

Bo was once invited to a strict, hard-shelled Baptist wedding of a prominent Midwestern family. No alcohol. The grooms-men, all gentlemen of the Southland, promptly devised a new drink: Café Jacques Danielle; it consisted of an ennsy-beensy dab of black coffee in a brimming cup of Jack Daniel's. The bride's mother called Bo over, and he thought he was done for. He just about ma'am-ed her to death. If you could be mauled with ma'ams, this lady would have had to go to the hospital. She was impressed. But she spoke her mind: "I worry about you young men—you drink too much coffee," she sighed. The moral is that with good manners and sufficient libations, you can have a Southern wedding in Idaho. His mama had taught him to be a gentleman.

Southerners never needed etiquette books in the past because all Southern towns had socially connected matrons who ruled the roost with an iron hand. In Greenville, one of these matrons was the late Louise Eskridge Crump, who worked—but it was okay because her job was being society editor at the *Democrat.* Another Greenville doyenne was Louise B. Mayhall, who was the society stringer for the *Memphis Commercial Appeal.* Although we pretend that we don't like publicity and that nice people are only in the newspaper when they are born and die, go off to camp, have a tea dance, get into the garden club, attend a meet-ing of the book club, or win a prize for the best pigs in the county at the 4-H club, we actually care a great deal about it, especially wedding write-ups. The local paper in the Crump era had four large spaces for pictures on the front of Sunday society pages, and Mrs. Crump dictated who got them. The best-connected bride got the upper left-hand corner on the Sunday front page. Anyplace on the page was considered good. We know a Memphis bride-to-be who got married, the first time, at least, during the hippie era. She nearly killed her poor mama by refusing to have a write-up in the Sunday paper. She relented, possibly because she did not want to go through life with the stigma of matricide attached to her name. By then all the good spots had been taken. Her big sister, a famous Memphis beauty and prominent matron, had to debase herself by calling the society editor. "Is she top-drawer?" the editor asked. "She's my sister," the matron replied. Hippie sister, of course, got the upper left-hand corner, and mama could hold up her head at the bridge club. Write-ups in the golden era of Mesdames Crump and Mayhall were decorous affairs: Initials were eschewed in favor of full names, and no chatty details, such as how the couple met at the Qwik Tyme car wash, were included; on the other hand, important pieces of information, such as the bride's direct line descent from Queen Elizabeth I, also known as the Virgin Queen, were.

While weddings in the Delta have always been major social events, in recent years some have taken on the patina of a pageant. Some are even more elaborate than the baton twirling at Mississippi State University, the kingpin twirling school. While Ole Miss is our premiere institution of higher learning, Mississippi State University, which inspires so much loyalty that one daughter moved to Europe so she wouldn't have to listen to her father talk about how NASA sends broken space shuttle doors to MSU to be repaired, has emerged as a very popular motif in Delta weddings. One groom's loyalty to his alma mater was reflected in a groom's cake baked in the shape of the MSU mascot, a bulldog. Grooms' cakes are a recent innovation with which we are not entirely comfortable—our rule of thumb is that anything that was not done in the past needn't to be done now. We are especially against a groom's cake that features a fishing tackle or golfing theme, or a replica of the groom's beloved Labrador retriever in a sleeping pose. Absolutely beyond the pale was the groom's cake surrounded with sugar-spun frogs, which, the write-up informed us, stood for "fully rely on God." We do fully rely on God, but we feel certain that He doesn't like bad taste any better than we do. One couple departed their reception at the country club in a golf cart to the accompaniment of MSU cowbells; cowbell favors were given to all the guests, who were encouraged to ring them in lieu of throwing rice (more on the rice issue later), but the big cowbell was rung by the groom's father. It was his own personal cowbell, a family keepsake, a gift from his father before him, which he had rung at numerous football games in the halcyon days when he studied animal husbandry at that fabled institution of higher learning. Cowbells have deep significance at State, but we ask: Is there such a thing as going too far?

As we peruse the eagerly awaited bride's issue of *Mississippi Magazine*—it features full-page color spreads on weddings and receptions—those of us who were blessed to be born in a better day sometimes find ourselves wondering: What would Mrs. Crump think? What, for example, might she make of the wedding write-up that put the name of the wedding planner in the second sentence, before naming the parents, the officiating clergyman, or the soloist who not only sang the Mississippi State University Fight Song, but also gave a beautiful reading of Philippians 2:9–11?

Many Delta wedding write-ups are more lethal than obituaries. A common fault is providing more detail than is, strictly speaking, necessary. One recent write-up featured the news that the five-layer wedding cake (with fondant icing that matched the lace on the bride's veil) had been specially made for the occasion in New York City, and that it had been "flown to town on an airplane." Like we thought it had walked or come on Trailways? But even the most tasteful write-up could not have saved a ranch-themed wedding in Rosedale, a small town that is justly famous for having the best dances in the Delta but in this instance flubbed badly. The bride and groom wore cowboy and cowgirl apparel, with the flower girl and ring bearer similarly attired. We don't think the E-ton suit comes in a cowboy cut. It had been coordinated by a planning company named Touch of Class. We think not.

Anybody with a touch of taste (we don't think it is nice to talk about c-l-a-s-s, even if we spend every waking hour thinking about it) would have told the groom that a horseshoe-shaped groom's cake was even worse than a fishing tackle groom's cake. Other refreshments included hogshead cheese (you don't want to know), crackling, and bowls of trail trash (see the recipe for White Trash, an elegant variation, on p. 164), stylishly served on tinfoil-covered trays. Is *trash* the operative word?

A Southern family is willing to go to the poorhouse for a nice wedding, and this doesn't just mean the mother of the bride. A notoriously penny-pinching father will join the Greenville Country Club just long enough to launch his Precious Baby with a lavish reception. If able, the Delta mother builds her entire house around her eldest daughter's wedding, even if the daughter hasn't been born when the first brick is laid and the first Ionic column reaches for the heavens. . . . Think garden reception. Planting the appropriate trees for a reception or, for the more ambitious, the wedding itself, takes a great deal of thought. Live oaks are lovely, but only if you're planning to skip a generation and wait for your granddaughter to wed. A good alternative is sweet olive bush, which in addition to being beautiful has a sweet fragrance, but not strong enough to drown out the bride's. Magnolias have the added merit of being the state flower and conjure up an image of moonlight and magnolias on the Delta. If the bride has a past and magnolias might remind somebody of her moonlight escapades, stick with something less likely to induce amorous thoughts. Boxwoods are nice, though nice people in the Delta say box rather than boxwood.

Although the Delta mother's allée, as she likes to call her double row of trees, is one of the most important concerns of her life, she forgets that, while she can dominate the wedding, she can't control nature. Here is an important rule about Delta weddings: Nature will not cooperate, Mother Nature being even more powerful and unappeasable than the Mother of the Bride (known as the MOB, and believe us, you'd rather deal with a mob boss than a MOB boss on her special day).

It is odd that we're always stunned by the torrential downpours that tend to greet the wedding morn, because, of course, we are an agrarian society. We should know better. Everybody in the Delta is in some way economically dependent on the workings of nature. Men in the Delta have tanned left arms from hanging out of their cars and pickups to observe the skies. When Percival Hampton, whose family had farmed in the Delta since before Lincoln was born, and who needed no further tutorials in seasonal transitions or downpour predicting, suffered financial reverses, he took to his bed—and watched the Weather Channel for three solid months. He was so glued to the Weather Channel that he refused to get out of bed and go to the dining room; his meals had to be sent back to him on a tray. "Your father is remarkable," his wife, Miss Lady Belle Hampton, chirped happily to her eldest daughter, Sistuh. "Any other man who'd been through what Percival has been through would have had a breakdown."

Torrential rains figure all too heavily in the sagas of many Delta weddings, including quite a few last Delta weddings. The Gordon Wilsons of Leland, Mississippi, had gone all out planning for a garden reception. Needless to say, it rained cats and dogs while the wedding party was on the way to witness the vows at the First Baptist Church in Greenville. Somebody had to rush to the casino over the levee and rent two buses. The Baptist church already had one bus. Even with three buses, somebody forgot to fetch the bride's grandmother—she has no immediate plans to forgive anybody, and we would guess that some will-changing has taken place.

Fortunately, the other little old ladies had more fun than a barrel of monkeys and loved being helped (read, shoved from the derriere) into the buses by young men. The Delta female never gets too old to appreciate the touch of a younger man. The old ladies grew giddier with every sip of champagne, which, along with the wine and hard liquor, was the only thing flowing harder than the rain. The Leland liquor store had to open up several times that night, starting at 9:30, when the bride's family first realized that they were on the brink of hosting a dry party—and nobody in the Delta wants a dry party, not dry in that sense anyway. Mr. Jim from the liquor store couldn't thank the Wilsons enough. He said the wedding was the reason for his wife's getting a new SUV for Christmas.

Then the electricity went out, and the Wilsons had to bring in generators, and two guests slipped on the hastily imported Astroturf and ended up in the swimming pool. But everybody had a good time, including the father of the bride, who did the Alligator (the Gator consists of lying on the floor and shaking—it is not unlike a mild convulsion. We reckon he had real convulsions when he toted up the bills). When the video came back, the family figured out why Mr. Jim from the liquor store had become, next to the groom, the most important man there: Half the Delta, many not recipients of an invitation, engraved or otherwise, could be seen gyrating on the dance floor.

Another Leland bride, whose wedding took place at St.

James' Episcopal Church in Greenville (the Leland Episcopal Church is too tiny for most Delta weddings, especially if it is the bride's first), held her reception on the old plantation. It was her family's plantation, the custom of renting scenic places for weddings not yet having made its way to the Delta. The house had been redone, including beige carpet in the living room. It was a three-tent wedding, which is the best kind in the Delta, more lavish by far than the mere two-tent or one-tent wedding. Everything was to be perfection itself, from the tiny little lamb chops, to the band from Memphis, naturally. Woodchips had been laid on the ground to make it easier to walk about and talk. We watched these very woodchips sinking into the mud. It rained buckets. The caterer wore knee boots, which was fortunate, as the mud came up to his calves. Still, it was a last Delta wedding— you saw everybody. When Bill Jessup had to dig his wife out of the mud that was sucking her to China, he used a silver spoon. That is what mattered, much more than the loss of the shoes, which were never found.

Frances Tuthill had spent her entire married life planning her daughter Eleanor's garden wedding. Every bulb had been procured, often at great expense and from foreign lands, with an eye to the wedding vista. On the morning of Eleanor's wedding, it was raining so hard that the allée looked like it was in the Amazon rain forest. Standing in the downpour, Miss Frances was gesturing wildly toward said allée when a solicitous cousin found her. "Eleanor will look so sweet walking down the allée this afternoon," she said. Well, not unless Eleanor rented a kayak. Finally, the cousin persuaded a reluctant Mrs. Tuthill to come in out of the rain. She called yet another cousin, and ordered, "Get over here and cut these bushes and get them to the Methodist church."

Despite the weather's refusal to bend to the will of a grand dame, even one who practically ran the garden club, the wedding came off beautifully. The rain stopped just in time for the reception, which was a blowout. We knew it would be long remembered as the last Delta wedding the next morning when we saw the wedding cake tilted on the breakfast room table and looking like the Leaning of Tower of Pisa. Notables from all over the South, splattered with mud, began straggling into the breakfast room around noon, soggy from a night spent in the gazebo. It had been a romantic Delta wedding—and not just for the bride and groom. It was one of those last Delta weddings that almost caused some first Delta divorces.

Frances Davenport Madison's Pound Cake

We don't want you to think that all Delta weddings, even ones that qualify as last Delta weddings, are big blowouts with a cast of thousands. This recipe makes a wonderful alternative wedding cake for a smallish wedding. We don't recommend groom's cakes, but we cannot say enough good things about this delicious cake. It came with a nice note from art curator George Shackelford, whose mother, Sue Shackelford, was a beloved lady who learned never to go out of the house without her gloves while finishing at the Ward Belmont School in Nashville. She was also the daughter of Mrs. Madison (1900–1991), whose specialty this was. "Here is the wonderful pound cake recipe, dug out of Sue's card files at Christmas in a bit of culinary archaeology," George wrote. "It really needs to be made when you are expecting enough people to mostly eat it up. Otherwise you end up at 3 A.M. in your underwear or nightgown in the kitchen sneaking just one more slice."

~~~~

Ingredients
3 cups flour
½ teaspoon baking powder
½ teaspoon salt
2 sticks butter
½ cup shortening

Preheat the oven to 325°.

Add the wet ingredients to the dry and blend to the consistency of corn meal. Then add

> *3 cups sugar*
> *5 eggs*

Blend, then add

> *1 cup milk*
> *1/2 teaspoon rum flavoring*
> *1/2 teaspoon coconut flavoring*

Blend, but avoid overworking the batter.

Place in a greased and floured Bundt pan.

Bake at 325° until the cake separates from the pan—about 1 hour.

Let cool for 10 minutes and remove from pan.

GLAZE

> *1/2 cup sugar*
> *1/4 cup water*

Boil and stir until thickened.

Add 1 teaspoon almond extract. Brush glaze on cake.

DELTA WEDDING BRUNCH FOR YANKEE GUESTS

OUR friend Hebe Randolph's family followed the custom of classically educated Southerners of former times in using names from Greek and Roman mythology. We only hope the first Hebe, the cupbearer to the immortals on Mount Olympus, had half as many china cups as our own Hebe, who is the umpteenth Hebe in her line. There are probably very few Yankees named Hebe (pronounced he-be). Hebe's niece did not marry a Yankee. But the niece lives in New York, and so a lot of the wedding guests had not previously visited the Mississippi Delta. We wanted them to get a real taste of the Delta.

We like to think they were impressed by the bonfires Hebe's brother built to help them find their way to the plantation (we also like to think our Delta bonfires are just like the ones they had in England when Prince Charles and Lady Di got hitched). Hebe lives on Deer Creek in Leland, Mississippi, about twelve miles from Greenville, and it is the perfect setting for a brunch for out-of-town guests. Disaster struck, however, when the caterer took sick. Bland Shackelford and Gayden jumped in at the last minute and saved the day. The wedding brunch was held the day of the wedding, which was an eight in the evening affair.

Pink and White Sauce for Oysters and Shrimp

Girls from the Delta love to use their stuff, and do they ever have the stuff. Gayden had two huge clamshells, together weighing in at four hundred pounds, in her backyard. She had taken a fancy to these clamshells and had them brought up from Florida. They were so heavy, the car listed. Not content with the damage done to one automobile, Gayden transported her enormous clamshells to Hebe's: the freshly shucked oysters and shrimp looked so pretty in their clamshells. (Please do not call this a raw bar.) The shells quickly sank into the gumbo (that's Delta for dirt). It looked like an oyster bar for a midget, not that we have anything against midgets, as long as they are refined. Finally, the table on which the clamshells sat had to be shored up with a plywood and brick base. Lemon halves were tied up with satin ribbons in little bags—of course, the lemons had been seeded first. Bland turned up her nose at the notion of red sauce at a wedding breakfast. But most of us have loved red sauce since we ate it on crackers as children. Still, a tasty white sauce or a pink, pink being perfect for a wedding breakfast, seemed more appropriate for a wedding brunch. The white sauce is simply home-made mayonnaise—which we pronounce mi-naise. (The clamshells were subsequently turned into birdbaths, and so we feel certain it was *their* last Delta wedding.)

PINK SAUCE

People in the Delta just love anchovies. Our friend Josie Winn used to call them "minnows." At the most famous restaurant in town, Doe's, the owner brings out a separate bowl of them for us to add to the salads. Lillo's, a popular restaurant a few miles from Greenville, is always obliged to add extra anchovies to their salads. They have a delicious pizza baked with lots of minnows. Not recommended for the bride within a week or two of the big day!

1 cup homemade mayonnaise
¾ cup bottled chili sauce
1 teaspoon anchovy paste
12 drops Tabasco
2 tablespoons tarragon vinegar

Mix all ingredients and chill one day before serving. Taste and adjust seasonings.

Makes about two cups.

WHITE SAUCE

A purist prefers a generous squeeze of lemon because it doesn't interfere with the taste of the oyster. This sauce, reflecting our deep and abiding love of mi-naise, is not for purists.

Ingredients
1 cup homemade mayonnaise
½ cup Durkee Famous Sauce
2 tablespoons Creole mustard
3 tablespoons chopped green onions
2 tablespoons horseradish (the jar variety found in the cooler
  section of the grocery)
1 tablespoon Lea & Perrins Worcestershire sauce
Juice of 1 lemon
1 teaspoon white pepper
Salt and Tabasco to taste

Combine all ingredients and chill overnight. Correct seasonings.

Makes one and a half cups.

Anne Hall Mcgee's Cheese Straws

Cheese straws are served at almost any occasion in the Delta. There are innumerable recipes, but this is the one that was used at Hebe's wedding brunch.

~~~~~

Ingredients
8 ounces sharp or extra-sharp Cheddar cheese
1 stick or little more butter, softened
2 scant cups sifted flour
1 teaspoon salt
Cayenne pepper to taste.

Preheat the oven to 375°.

Grate cheese in processor. Let sit until room temp, add butter. Mix in flour, salt, and cayenne to taste depending on how hot and spicy you want the cheese straws to be. Hot and spicy is best. Fill cookie press fitted with ribbon disk and press onto cookie sheet. Bake at 375° for about 12 minutes.

Makes about six dozen.

Alsha Mccourt's Bloody Marys by the Gallon

At the brunch, these were served with a celery stalk garnish.

~~~~

2½ cans (28 ounces) V8 juice
Juice of 2 limes and 2 lemons (lemons optional)
2 heaping tablespoons horseradish
1 teaspoon celery salt
¼ cup Lea & Perrins Worcestershire sauce
2 teaspoons Tabasco
1 teaspoon black pepper
2 teaspoon Cavender's Greek seasoning
2 cloves crushed garlic
1 beef boullion cube dissolved in ¼ cup water
Vodka—not less than a fifth, but Deltans prefer a liter.

Mix all ingredients and stir.

Makes one gallon.

Venison Grillades

This was an unusual treat for visitors from New York—and for us. "I had never had this dish until my sister-in-law, Martha Green, brought it up here from South Louisiana," recalls Bland. "I was having a dear friend who lives in England for brunch and wanted to serve something local. My husband, Johnny, had a freezer full of venison hams and so began the experiment. After consulting lots of books, we found a recipe we liked, and tinkered with it." Grillades, by the way, is a stew with a fancy French name. Like a pot roast, grillades can be cooked forever to good advantage. Served over grits (recipe below).

SEASONED FLOUR

1 cup all-purpose flour
2 teaspoons freshly ground black pepper
1 teaspoon freshly ground white pepper
1 teaspoon cayenne

Mix in a bowl and put aside.

GRILLADES

4 pounds venison ham
6 or more tablespoons bacon fat
2 cups chopped scallions

1 cup chopped red onion
¾ cup chopped celery
2 sliced red bell peppers
2 or 3 large cloves fresh garlic
4 cups beef stock
1½ cups red wine
3 tablespoons tomato paste
3 teaspoons salt
1 teaspoon Tabasco

BOUQUET GARNI

3 bay leaves
6 sprigs fresh thyme
6 sprigs fresh parsley

Tie the bouquet garni ingredients in a bundle.

Preheat the oven to 350°.

Cut the meat in large strips, about three inches long and about an inch wide. Season the flour with salt. Dip strips in flour, but do not dip all at once, as they will get soggy. Heat a Dutch oven until hot. Add the bacon grease. Start with the meat that is ready, and brown. Keep going until all the meat is done. Lift the meat out of the Dutch oven and put it in a bowl. Scrape the Dutch oven, and add the vegetables. Cook, stirring, until the onions are clear. Put the meat back into the Dutch oven, adding the stock, wine, tomato paste, and bouquet garni. Place a piece of parchment paper between the lid and the pan for a perfect seal and then put the Dutch oven into the oven and heat at 350° for 2 hours. Check, and if the meat is not falling apart, put it back for another hour. Do this until it is fork-tender. Adjust the seasonings and season to taste with Tabasco. This is better after a day in the icebox (as we call the refrigerator). Bland and Gayden highly recommend that you lift the fat if it has been refrigerated.

Serves twenty.

GRITS

PLEASE do not think of the grits as just something to put under the grillades. There is a Southern mystique about grits. "Here is what I know to be true about grits," says Bland, who goes all Brillat-Savarin on us when the sacred subject of grits is broached. "DO NOT BUY, no matter what anyone says, instant or quick cooking grits. You are doomed to failure if you buy these abominations. Delta Grind, Arrowhead, or any stone-ground grits are what you are after. You can safely follow the recipe on the package. If you like, you can cook grits well ahead and put them in a bain marie [or water bath]—put the container of grits in a larger container filled halfway with hot water. This will keep the grits warm until they are served. Put them in the water bath, stick a fork in about a tablespoon of butter, and run that butter all over the surface of the grits. This prevents a skin from forming. A skin on grits is entirely unacceptable. You can spray some Saran Wrap with Pam and put it on top of the butter if it is going to be a really long time. If they get too thick while you are waiting to serve, whisk in some really hot water until they are the right consistency. Start with a cup of water if you have a really big pot.

"Always, always, always put the salt in the water first.

continued

You can never get the salt right if you do not. You come out with much less salt than if you try to fix it at the end.

"Being a grits purist, I cook them in water, but I am told you can use chicken stock, beef stock, or add milk or cream at the end."

BUTTER MOLD

SOUTHERNERS love butter. We think that the three main food groups are sugar, salt, and fat. We love any heart-healthy dish that blends all three. If we didn't stop him, Harley Metcalfe IV ate butter like a Popsicle when he was a child. We call this naked butter. But we thought that an elegant butter mold would be better for a wedding brunch. We use Land O Lakes (unsalted) because that is the best butter available down here. A self-confessed food snob, Bland makes jaunts to Little Rock to procure finer brands, but Land O Lakes works very well.

Soften 2 pounds of unsalted butter and then process it in your food processor until it is smooth. Pack it in a mold, being careful not to leave air pockets, and put it in the icebox. To unmold, run a hot knife around the sides of the mold and put a warm dish towel on the top—it will slide right out and be lovely. We used a heart-shaped mold.

Cranberry Chutney

We garnished the butter mold with this. It makes a nice tart
butter . . . accompaniment for grits and grillades.

~~~~

Ingredients
1 cup sultanas (raisins)
1/2 cup bourbon
3 twelve-ounce bags (fresh) cranberries
2 1/4 cups sugar
1 1/2 navel oranges, thinly sliced and seeded
1/2 lemon, thinly sliced and seeded
1/2 cup water
1 two-inch piece fresh ginger, peeled and chopped
2 cloves chopped garlic
1 cinnamon stick

Soak sultanas in bourbon until plumped, or for at least thirty
minutes. Cook cranberries, plumped sultanas (and any leftover
bourbon), sugar, orange slices, and lemon slices in the water until cranberries begin to pop. Add ginger, garlic, and cinnamon
stick to the mixture. Stir, put lid on pan, and let the chutney rest:
The flavors will become friendly.

Makes six half-pint jars.

Milk Punch

Ingredients
1 box (1 pound) cofectioners' sugar
4 tablespoons vanilla
1 gallon milk
1 fifth bourbon
Freshly ground nutmeg

Add the sugar and vanilla to the milk. Stir in bourbon (after having a sip or two to be sure it's good bourbon).

Freeze overnight and thaw a bit the next morning so that the consistency is slushy.

Sprinkle with nutmeg.

Serves twenty-five.

Wedding Brunch Salad

At either end of the dining room table, there were matching silver trays. The salad was served on one (a flat surface is outstanding for such a beautiful salad). The other tray held two chafing dishes, one for grits and the other for grillades. One must never put a chafing dish on a table without a tray! Sterno doesn't bring out the best in wood.

SALAD

Mixed greens
Fresh grapefruit segments
Fresh orange segments
Pomegranate seeds
Avocado slices

DRESSING

¾ cup good olive oil
2 to 3 tablespoons fresh grapefruit juice
Splash of balsamic vinegar
½ teaspoon salt
Freshly ground black pepper

We composed the greens and gently incorporated the fruit. The dressing was lightly tossed into the salad.

Dorothy's Biscuits

We used a silver biscuit box—that wasn't a great idea because Dorothy's biscuits are so delicious, we had to refill the smallish box constantly. But form over function. The table was lovely!

One more important note on biscuits: Smaller is better. These are small and fluffy, and you can add a dash of cream of tartar to make them even fluffier. Big chunky biscuits are called cat head biscuits. Think of these as fingerling biscuits.

✦✦✦✦

Ingredients
2 cups flour
1 teaspoon salt
2 teaspoons sugar
4 teaspoons baking powder
¼ teaspoons cream of tartar
5 heaping tablespoons shortening
1 cup whole milk

Preheat the oven to 400°.

Mix dry ingredients, cut in shortening with a fork, stir in milk. Roll out on floured surface ½ inch thick. Cut with small (1½-inch diameter) biscuit cutter with fluted edge. Place on ungreased cookie sheet, and prick tops gently three times with a fork. Bake at 400° about 18–20 minutes or until lightly browned. If necessary, you may brown quickly under the broiler.

Makes about thirty-five biscuits.

Pecan Tassies

Adapted from *A Cook's Tour of Shreveport*, the cookbook of the Junior League of Shreveport, Louisiana, this recipe was selected as the perfect Southern dessert to serve to invaders from the north.

CREAM CHEESE PASTRY

> *3 ounces cream cheese*
> *1/2 cup butter*
> *1 1/4 cup sifted flour*

FILLING

> *3/4 cup brown sugar*
> *1 tablespoon soft butter*
> *1 teaspoon grated orange peel*
> *1/2 teaspoon orange extract*
> *Dash salt*
> *1 egg, beaten*
> *2/3 cup coarsely broken pecans*

Preheat the oven to 350°.

Put flour in food processor, mix in cream cheese and butter until dough ball forms. Shape into a disk, wrap in plastic, and chill at least 1 hour. Pinch off small pieces of dough, flatten in the palm of your hand, and press into ungreased mini muffin cups. It should fill 24 cups.

Mix together all the filling ingredients except the pecans. Divide half the pecans among the pastry-lined cups, add 1 teaspoon of the egg mixture and top with the remaining pecans. Bake at 350° for 25 minutes or until filling is set. Cool and remove from pans. They may be frozen or made ahead.

Makes twenty-four.

Greenville Planter's Punch

This planter's punch is from a privately published cook-book by the aforementioned Louise B. Mayhall, whose name was synonymous with weddings. Mrs. Mayhall was famous for making a blue garter, the something blue, for brides—but only for brides who got good placement in the newspaper. Just kidding.

~~~~

Ingredients
1 tablespoon confectioners' sugar
Juice of one lemon
½ ounce rum
½ ounce bourbon whisky
1 ounce brandy
Carbonated water

Shake all ingredients except water with ice and stir in a julep cup with ice cubes. Fill with carbonated water and stir.

This is the recipe for one good drink—and it's not for sissies.

2

⌇⌇⌇⌇

Finding the Groom:
Is He One of the Clarksdale Clarks?

As NECESSARY AS the groom might be for the proper Delta wedding, a Southern girl must never—nevuh!—be congratulated upon obtaining one. To do so is an insult to Southern womanhood. It hints that the bride has caught, rather than been caught. The proper form is to congratulate the groom and wish the bride-to-be happiness. This chivalrous convention must be observed if the bride is destined to give birth to a surprisingly large preemie immediately after the last "I do." Congratulating the bride is the height of rudeness, and rude is the worst epithet there is in the Delta. When Jane Allen Tolliver was mugged on a trip to New Orleans, she pronounced it "just about the rudest thing that ever happened."

The groom is inevitably underfoot on the day of the wedding, but he must be tolerated, while the bride, her mother, and—a distant third—his mother soak up the limelight. The two mothers, if not already best friends, either bond for life or develop a lifelong enmity during the negotiations over who gets to wear what color—you can't have the two leading matrons in the same pastel shade. The mothers' entrance into the church, breathlessly awaited by all, far outshines the groom's. The groom's mother is supposed to wear beige and be nice—that means quiet. Her son's job is to pay the minister—and to say, "I do." His parents are responsible for the rehearsal dinner, and being unobtrusive—and if possible presentable. One snobbish mother was distraught that her daughter was marrying the son of an elevator operator. Mrs. Silly Snoot put it in the write-up in the *Democrat* that the father of the groom was a "vertical engineer."

The groom at most hopes not to embarrass himself too much on his wedding day. This is not as easy as it sounds. He may be kidnapped or have his unmentionables painted with purple impetigo medicine that glows. Dead fish may be hung from the hibiscus in his mother's yard. At St. James' Episcopal Church, at other times a Delta-wide symbol of ceremonial perfection, the groomsmen inevitably find it hilarious to steal his shoes and paint "Save" on the sole of the groom's left shoe and "Me" on the bottom of the other one. When the unsuspecting bridegroom kneels, the entire church is filled with refined giggles. You'd think St. James' grooms would learn to check their shoes, but they don't. It works every time. A Presbyterian groom faced another peril at St. James': He started reciting his vows in a heavy English accent, unconsciously imitating the rector's. No, the rector wasn't an Englishman. A pretend English accent is the Episcopal minister's version of speaking in tongues. The rector had been a star in his seminary's English accent workshop.

Sometimes a bridegroom fails at even the most minimal of tasks set for him. For example, it is bad luck for the groom to see the bride on the day of the wedding before she walks up the aisle, a resplendent vision of Southern womanhood. An inconsiderate groom may approach his lady on the day of the festivities, setting off loud shrieks from the bride, her mother, and all the distaff side of the wedding party. Southern women just love to shriek, and if you can't abide this, marry a Yankee. Which brings us to Billy Cushing, a Yankee bridegroom; he also happened to be a Catholic. Naturally Billy insisted upon being married at St. Joe's, the Catholic church in Greenville. A gothic gem on Main Street, it was the perfect setting for a wedding. Olivia Morgan, who proudly called herself "a convent girl," because the convent figured in the long list of schools to which her conscientious but ultimately defeated parents had sent her, always urged people to bundle up if they were headed to St. Joe's. "It's cold as flugeons in there," she would aver knowledgeably, using a Southern expression the precise meaning of which is lost, and always adding meaningfully, "And those people hold forth longer than Baptists." But this was a summer wedding, and the church was decked out beautifully; of course, some of the bride's friends almost flipped when they noticed the plastic rosaries the statues were "wearing." They suggested going to Farnsworth's on Washington Avenue to buy nicer "jewelry" for the tackily dressed Christian saints. It seems that poor Billy's job was complicated by Father Igoe, much-loved and stone deaf. Father Igoe was subsequently killed on the railroad track by a train he never heard coming. But back to the wedding. As usual, Father Igoe couldn't hear the vows. Billy became so frustrated he shouted, "I do! I do! I do!" as we tittered nervously.

Sistuh Girl Gibson, the bride, was not Catholic. Although willing to submit to Catholic nuptials, she had a set-to with Father Igoe over the wedding veil. He insisted she don this symbol of womanly purity, but Sistuh Girl—living symbol of other aspects of Southern womanliness—refused. Father Igoe may have been deaf as a post, but he was not blind, and you should have seen his face when a veil-less Sistuh Girl started up the aisle on the arm of her father. "At least," a Delta wag not unacquainted with Sistuh Girl's particular brand of joie de vivre noted approvingly, "she was true to herself."

We should mention that the Delta boasts several aristocratic old Catholic families. The Plunketts, for example, were early settlers of Washington County, where Greenville, the hub of the universe, is located. They claim descent from P. G. T. Beauregard, the great Creole general. His bloody (or was it rusty?) sword hung on their landing. Old Mrs. Plunkett must have been tempted to use it on Henriette (please don't pronounce the H— P.G.T. wouldn't have) after she climbed down a ladder from her fine Catholic girls' boarding school into the arms of not just a waiting Baptist, but a waiting Baptist preacher.

Another important task of the groom: providing the biggest engagement ring he can possibly afford. A Southern girl dreams of being able to nonchalantly extend her left hand, blinding, and ask, "How is mah finger like a lemon pie? [Pause.] 'Cause I got mah ring on it." She hopes that you will be blinded by her ring and, if you are one of her dearest friends, also by envy. So does her mother. "You never want your daughter to come home with an engagement ring she could wear safely on the New York subway," summed up one matron, indicating that perhaps the Delta mother is not entirely lacking in predatory skills.

In the takes-one-to-know-one category, the mother has taught her daughter that the male of the species is a fairly simple creature who enjoys the challenge of hunting small birds, large deer, and hard-to-get women. A hard-to-get girl knows to always get off the phone first and never accept a date later than Wednesday. Something else that brings out the Delta male's hunting instincts—her daddy owns a farm with all-new John Deere equipment on the sandy loam banks of Deer Creek, the richest soil in the Delta. Think of it as a dowry.

An engagement ring is just the beginning, though, fortunately for the groom, he doesn't have to supply the rest of his beloved's humble material requirements—at least initially. The bride will be competing with her own siblings to get grandmother's flat silver and Mama's hollowware. Every Southern town has a jewelry store of choice. Farnsworth's was always ours, though it was perfectly acceptable to shop at Schloms. Farnsworth's, however, had a consultant to help the bride select china and silver patterns. In the old days, the late lamented Brodnax Jewelers or Julius Goodman, another now-defunct store in Memphis, which did silver pattern exchanges, were even more desirable. That faulty line of thinking still exists today: Whatever you find in Memphis or New Orleans or Atlanta is far superior.

A Delta girl always looks for generosity in a man. When Bub Avery, a leading light in the local construction industry, fell madly in love with Anne Epps Highsmith, who lived in the country on a dirt road, he thought he knew how to win her heart: "I'll pour you a four-lane highway out to your house," he vowed, perhaps not unaware that the road would make his courting easier. This was tempting, and just the kind of indication of prosperity a Delta girl appreciates. Anne Epps had been hot to trot for quite a while. Still, she rejected his suit and became engaged to the boy from the next farm over, a lifelong friend. No four-lane highway needed—and her diamond ring was so big that, if she dropped it on any road, it could puncture the tire of a pickup truck.

The Delta bride frequently searches the world over—at least as far as Jackson or Memphis—for her ideal husband and then chooses the boy next door. We'd be hard-pressed to name all the Delta husbands who carried their wives' schoolbooks in third grade. Boys from outside the Delta sometimes don't understand us, and, when they visit, get culture shock. We'll never forget the look on one young man's face when he came down from the University of Virginia to visit his girlfriend. One of our more fun-loving matrons fell into the bottle and got knee-walking drunk at a party. When no longer able to walk—on her hands *or* knees—she collapsed spread-eagled on the living room floor. The beau glowered. Whatever happened to the cavalier tradition? We drove him to the airport bright and early the next morning, a vein in his temple throbbing. Culture shock is not uncommon when Delta girls bring suitors home.

Anne Epps took her search even farther afield than Memphis. She went to London. Her mission seemed to be to show how much fun colonials have. However, we could tell that she was making a huge mistake when she took her fine English beau to the dingiest bar in the French Quarter and proceeded to jump onto the tabletops and dance the night away with jolly jack-tars from a naval installation. It was apparent that the colonies weren't making quite the right impression we'd hoped on Anthony Lloyd-Boyd. We were just devastated that Anne Epps didn't get to become Lady Lloyd-Boyd. We were already planning to be the toast of London, what with our cute accents. We were going to slay the noble lords and ladies by speaking Lelanese, the most exaggerated Delta accent, indigenous to Leland, Mississippi.

One of the best ways to find the right man is to marry Mother's best friend's son. This ensures "a similar background." That is Delta for "of the same social class." You have to telegraph messages on this subject—e.g., if your daughter brings home the wrong boy, don't say he's not as well bred as Daddy's hunting dog Fang Jr.—simply pretend he's not present. He will get the message the third time you get his name wrong. A Delta mother, even today, wants a bridegroom from a fine family with old money (or, failing that, a rich family with lots of shiny new money). When one girl was having boyfriend problems, her mother told everybody in town that he was just plumb tacky— and so were his parents, grandparents, and all other antecedents. The couple became engaged the next day; Mother had to pile in her car and drive the length and breadth of Greenville explaining that her new son-in-law-to-be was descended from a famous Civil War general. You can't be too careful: One paragon of motherhood in Alabama wrote the governor of Mississippi, whom she had never met, to inquire after her daughter's fiancé's lineage. We shudder to think what might have happened if the perplexed governor, who had not heretofore regarded himself as being in the matchmaking business, had not called him "a nice young man." Needless to say, the groom's family never entirely forgave her.

Delta mothers develop creative ways to dispose of what they regard as an unsuitable match. In addition to ignoring him, she may indicate that the girl's family will no longer be able to defray the cost of the bride's education and that the burden will fall upon his young shoulders. The mother must be able to avail herself of an unexpected opportunity. Timidly asked by the mother of a son courting Anne Dudley if alcoholism ran in the Dudley line, Big Anne jumped at the chance: "Rampant!" she practically screamed. She dwelt at length on Uncle Timothy's DTs and the time Uncle Billy gave away his farm to the church in a blackout. In no time flat, the would-not-be mother-in-law had plenty of ammunition. Big Anne didn't even have to drop the hint that the boy's family might have to take up Anne Dudley's tuition at the fashion institute.

Oddly enough, the Delta mother does not tell her daughters about sex. "I just talk hypothetically," purrs one Delta mother. "I say things like, 'I could practically get pregnant every time your daddy looked at me.'" In the Delta, this is known as telling your daughter the facts of life in graphic detail. "If you ever want to know about sex," a married big sister told her little sister, "call me collect. I'm not sure Mama knows." Yet—somehow—the Delta girl *does* know. She is born knowing how to wrap herself around a man so fast that the boa constrictor ought to take lessons from her. Like the boa constrictor, she may toy with or tease her prey mercilessly before zeroing in for the kill. Unlike the boa constrictor, she knows when to stop. Generally. "Why buy the cow if you can get the milk for free?" is a mantra she has heard all her life. The only other real difference between the Delta girl and the boa constrictor is that the boa constrictor doesn't want a diamond ring. Mothers of boys constantly warn their sons not to fall into the arms of a boa constrictor, the kind of boa constrictor that has a ring finger.

A chapter about a groom, as you can see, is really about the bride's mother. Mother is deeply involved in a daughter's search for the right young man, as you may be gathering. Olivia Morgan Gilliam's mother even wrote her love letters for her. This was a practice that foreshadowed Miss Olivia's habit of enlisting her brainy sister-in-law to write her reviews for the book club. She resigned when her sister-in-law refused to write one more book review. Old Mrs. Gilliam's love letters were such gems that two of Olivia's beaux compared their billet doux on a long train trip. They were not amused to discover that the missives were identical. They confronted Olivia Morgan. Old Mrs. Gilliam was outraged: the very idea of a gentleman showing a lady's letter! That is what she wrote in Olivia's identical replies to the young reprobates. Both cads apologized.

Much to the chagrin of Delta parents, all too many girls go

through a honky-tonk angel phase during which they dance their feet off with gallant young rednecks at juke joints. It's a lot of fun. Unfortunately, some get engaged before emerging from this period. The great-great-granddaughter of a governor (not the one who found himself providing marital references) did this. The family was beside itself, except for Great-Aunt Isabell, who had a thing for rakes. She even forgave the boy for sitting in the governor's chair and shattering it to smithereens. When the wedding took place, the church was a sight: On one side were ladies in pantsuits with what is known as the "Pentecostal do"— it's bigger than regular big hair—and on the other were tamer "helmet heads" and funereal facial expressions, except for Aunt Isabell, who was giddy. "You didn't need an usher," said one guest, "to tell you which side was the groom's side."

Sometimes the Delta mother is torn when it comes to marrying off her pride and joy: On the one hand, she wants a fine young man from a fine old family who is planning to build a big fine house right next door to her. In her heart of hearts, she thinks it is a good idea to wait until the right man comes along. On the other hand, she is eager to have a big party, the sooner the better. Mrs. Pritchett from Rosedale got so carried away with the notion of being the first mother in the Delta to have an outdoor champagne fountain at the reception that she insisted on having the big event when it was practically freezing. She was determined that her fountain would kick off the bridal season and thereby garner a prominent place in write-ups in *Memphis Commercial Appeal*. A champagne fountain can be tricky, especially if the family is hard-shell Baptists. We'll never forget the

Baptist family who substituted peach punch, made from canned peaches, for champagne—it clogged the valves of the fountain and guests were forced to dodge sporadic blasts of shooting peach glop. If you're going to have a champagne fountain, have real champagne, the best you can afford. Bad champagne gives you a bad hang hang, as Delta girls like to say. Another sign that you're at a Baptist wedding: Not only is the "champagne" really lime sherbet, but the mints, bridesmaids' dresses, and cream cheese sandwiches are all dyed to match it.

A wedding is so important to the Southern mother that she attends other weddings solely to spy. She feels she must check up on what other mothers have done. Sometimes you get the impression that a Southern mother is so eager to have a big wedding that she will marry off Little Baby Dahlin' to just about anybody—a Yankee, an obvious peckerwood (different from the plain vanilla redneck in that the peckerwood traditionally resides in a mobile home), or a closet queen. That last will initially delight the manners-obsessed Southern mother-in-law: He is so sweet that he takes an interest in the bridesmaids' dresses and pronounces po' de crème correctly. One such groom-to-be came to his senses and moved to the French Quarter in New Orleans in lieu of getting hitched at the First Baptist Church. He had picked the bride's Vera Wang dress himself, and for a dreadful moment, we thought he'd taken it with him.

One of the most fertile (please, *not* that way—this was the 1950s) hunting grounds for the Delta belle to find a marriageable beau was the Greenville Air Force Base. We'd be hard-pressed to estimate how many girls might have become old-maid school teachers, not that there's anything wrong with this, if not for the base. This was in the era of the dashing young cadet—there were dashing lieutenants, officers, and gentlemen, who often had attended schools even better than State or Ole Miss. And how did the Greenville girl make the acquaintance of these young flyer boys? Well, tea dances, of course. The tea dance is an even more genteel version of the ballroom dance, held in the afternoon. Miss Ethel Payne, who worked at the base and was the daughter of one of Greenville's most beloved doctors, organized the dances. She got literally hundreds of Delta girls married off. Several local lasses ended up marrying into prominent families, thanks to Uncle Sam's putting the air base in Greenville—and Miss Payne, for putting the boys and girls together in an irreproachably refined setting. In addition to Miss Payne's tea dances, there were less genteel boogies at the hangar, where a swing musician named Charlie Barnett played—these dances were known as "swing and sweat with Charlie Barnett." We feel certain the girls at Miss Payne's tea dances did not sweat—they glowed (genteel for "perspire").

The best thing about dating a boy from the base, by the way, is that, if he was a pilot, he could buzz your house. This consisted in risking his life to fly low enough to shake everything in the house. We considered it the height of sophistication and wit. If a Delta girl's house shook like the Russians had just dropped a bomb (and in that era we worried that they might, the bridge across the Mississippi River being so important and all), it meant you had a date that night.

Whatever the closing of the air base did to the economy of

Greenville and the entire Delta, far worse, it eliminated a lot of good marriage possibilities. But it was good while it lasted. The colonel who ran the base is now a squire in Leland—which means that one more Leland girl found a mate. Some of the young men, of course, had to be educated in our ways—one who married at St. James' forgot to give the rector an honorarium and had to mail it back, but he sent it to the wrong church. And we thought he was such a prize because he was a graduate of W. Nell (Washington and Lee, to you)! His mistake, however, was easily rectified—or should we say rectorfied? The Presbyterian minister handed it over to the redoubtable rector at the next Rotary lunch.

Dancing has always had a mystique in the Delta—we'd hate to think of all the mismatched couples that initially got together because of a shared love of dancing. Girls and boys were sent to Mrs. Pinckney's ballroom dance classes, held in the same community center hallowed by Miss Payne's tea dances. They spent the afternoon dancing to "Sewanee River Rock," which was already about twenty years out of date by the time Mrs. Pinckney heard about it, and drinking imaginary punch from the imaginary punch bowl. Still, acquiring ballroom skills is worth the effort. Ladies in their eighties still reminisce about the length of their stag lines. Miss Olivia Morgan, who always got a misty look in her eyes when she spoke of stag lines, confessed her secret trick: She whispered the name of her favorite song to all the boys, flirtatiously hinting that she'd love to dance with them when it was played. "My stag lines wrapped around the ballroom floor," she recalled in old age. In fact, those may have been her last words on her deathbed.

Not all Delta girls have such happy memories. Alice Hunt, who has two left feet, says that she moved to New York partly to avoid going to dances. "I spent my youth pretending to powder my nose in country clubs around the Delta," she still recalls sourly. Alice Hunt apparently felt that being a powder-room flower was less humiliating than being a wallflower. Other girls locked themselves in bathroom stalls and stood on top of the commodes so nobody could see their feet. Dare we call them commode flowers?

Although no longer able to avail herself of the air base, the Delta girl would not be caught dead using Match.com, the Internet dating service used by apparent hussies elsewhere. Have these women no pride? Are they not NICE? Are they . . . ugly? Of course, the Delta girl doesn't need Match.com. She has her own, state-supported Match.com: It is called Ole Miss. At Ole Miss, the Delta girl pursues advanced placement courses in laughing, drinking, and hair flipping. For some unknown reason, hair flipping drives Southern boys wild. In addition to mastering the art of the flip, joining the right sorority is crucial. A sorority will have a special relationship with various fraternities, and your choice of a sorority may well influence whom you marry. The gentlemanly hell-raisers of SAE tend to make a beeline for the proud Chi Omegas. Tri-Delts are nice and not as haughty as Chi Os. They love to answer the sorority house phone, "This is Delta, Delta, Delta, can I hep you, hep you, hep you?" Before marrying a Tri-Delt, a man should ask himself a question: Would she drive me nuts, nuts, nuts?

Ole Miss isn't the only state school that specializes in charm—and academics, too, of course. There is also the W—as the much-beloved former Mississippi State College for Women was affectionately known. It is now Mississippi University for Women ("and a few good men," the college's T-shirt brags—the few men being in the nursing department, which probably means you'd do better looking for a beau at State. On second thought, a male nurse might be ideal for a Delta girl, as nobody in the world takes being waited on better than the Delta girl). When Lamar Hitchcock, a particularly successful graduate, having a handsome husband and, something extra, a job, was invited to speak at career day, her panel was assigned a topic: "What I learned at the W." As her turn to speak drew nearer, Lamar became more and more agitated. Just what, if anything, *had* Lamar learned at the W? English literature? Trigonometry? Well, perhaps not. Then a light went on in her head: She *had* learned something at the W. She had learned how to button and unbutton a coat properly, and the art of ascending and descending stairs gracefully. If you can count, that's actually *two* things Lamar had learned while "studying" at the W. (You must always button from the top down and do the opposite when unbuttoning your coat; we don't know why. When going up or down the steps, you must turn your knees every so slightly toward the banister; this way they won't look splayed.) These were among the precepts taught in what was once the W's only required course: charm class. "You might be able to get out without history or English," Lamar says wistfully, "but not without the charm class."

Another good place to look for a husband is church or Bible study. Our dear friend Anne Dudley—who has accepted no fewer than five proposals of holy matrimony—found number three at Episcopal Bible study. You might have two immediate reactions to this news. First: Maybe you didn't know Episcopalians read the Bible—isn't it for Methodists and Baptists? Second: You might have thought a young buck from Bible study would be a safe bet. Well, you couldn't be more wrong—at least on the second point. We'll just leave it at that, in case that good-for-nothing Orval is still living. But here's the caveat: Always be especially careful of any man you meet in Bible study. This goes double for Bible salesmen, as some of the most hell-raising boys in the Delta traditionally get summer jobs selling Bibles door-to-door.

But sometimes a house of worship is just the ticket, if not to heaven, to spouse hunting. Old Man Stith, who was Young Man Stith back then, had excellent luck at the tiny Episcopal church in Glen Allen, Mississippi. He was visiting Mississippi and just naturally wanted to go to church—he was probably settling in for his usual sermon snooze, when a young lady, sailing up the aisle to take her place, caught his eye. Turning to a friend, he said: "Introduce me to that young lady, and you can be the best man at my wedding." "No," said the friend, "she is already engaged to be married—to me." Still, the friend foolishly introduced Mr. Stith to his fiancée. Mr. Stith was invited to tea that very afternoon and in no time flat, his friend's fiancée had a new fiancé—Old Man Stith.

SUNDAY LUNCH TO IMPRESS
A PROSPECTIVE BRIDEGROOM

Leg of Lamb

A pampered Southern belle may not actually be planning to do much in the way of cooking meals once she is married. But that doesn't mean Mother can't serve a mouthwatering Sunday dinner. She may gently, if not always honestly, hint that Little Baby Dahlin' helped her with the meal. We think lamb is the height of elegance, a dish to which the male seems intuitively responsive.

This recipe is for a 7-pound (or as close as possible) leg of lamb.

~~~~

Ingredients
1 cup freshly squeezed lemon juice
¾ cup olive oil
Grated zest of two lemons
3 cloves garlic, minced
½ cup chopped parsley
2 tablespoons dried oregano
1 tablespoon sea salt
2 teaspoons freshly ground pepper
1 or 2 sprigs fresh rosemary

The day before serving, combine lemon juice and olive oil. Add the lemon zest, garlic, parsley, oregano, salt, and pepper. Whisk until incorporated.

Score the lamb and pour the marinade into the cuts. Put the rosemary sprigs on top of the lamb, cover the container, and marinate overnight.

Bring the lamb to room temperature and grill until pink. Remember that the meat will continue to cook when taken off the fire.

Do not overcook! Lamb is better when closer to the rare/pink side. When overcooked, it is tough and tasteless.

Serves eight to ten.

Grandmother's Mint Sauce

Ingredients
1 cup vinegar
2 tablespoons sugar (some people like confectioners')
2 tablespoons mint leaves, chopped

In a small saucepan, bring all ingredients to a boil. Simmer a few minutes.

Strain and serve in a sauce dish garnished with a sprig of fresh mint. Unfortunately, the color is not good. You might consider adding (horrors) a touch of green food coloring.

A little dab will do you.

Makes about a cup.

Mother's Mint Sauce

Ingredients
4 apples
½ cup confectioners' sugar
Fresh mint leaves
1 teaspoon Dry Sack
Lemon slice

Quarter the apples. Put the apples in a saucepan and barely cover with water. Cook (covered) until the apples are very soft, about 40 minutes. Remove from the heat.

Drain and reserve the juice. You should have a cup of apple juice. Add confectioners' sugar and bring the juice/sugar mixture to a boil. Reduce heat and cook until the mixture thickens. Mother's always turned a light golden brown, at which point she added ⅓ cup of chopped mint leaves. She would put the leaves in a measuring cup and use kitchen shears to snip, bruising the leaves to emit more flavor. Return to heat and cook about ten minutes more. Remove from stove and allow to sit a minute or two.

Strain the syrup, pushing on the leaves to get as much juice and flavor from the mint as possible. Add 1 teaspoon Dry Sack and 1 slice lemon (squeeze the juice out). As this sauce turns out to be rather golden in color, it's nice to add a sprig of fresh mint and a lemon slice just before serving.

Makes one cup.

Third-Generation Mint Sauce or Newlywed Mint Sauce

We use Crosse & Blackwell jelly because that's what we can get down here, and it was our mothers' and grandmothers' designer choice, upscale you know.

~~~~

Ingredients
1 jar (12 ounces) red currant jelly
2 tablespoons finely minced mint leaves
1 tablespoon freshly grated orange rind

Melt the currant jelly over low heat. Add the mint leaves and the orange rind. Allow to sit until cool. Then refrigerate until serving time, overnight if possible.

Makes one and a half cups.

Fresh Asparagus with Hollandale Sauce

We know you call it hollandaise sauce—but Harley Metcalfe likes to call it Hollandale sauce in honor of Hollandale, Mississippi. Not everyone knows where Hollandale, Mississippi, is, but are they ever missing out. It is a small community of about 7,000 souls, three-quarters of whom are excellent cooks and hostesses.

Fresh asparagus bears little resemblance to the canned variety. We love the tiniest, thinnest spears possible. If you grow your own, you probably won't get that beautiful, thin variety. Therefore, you must (after washing) take a potato peeler and peel about halfway up the stem. If you are fortunate and you get the thin version in your garden, then you can simply snap the stems off. I prefer to peel my asparagus.

Place the prepared asparagus in boiling water and cook for about 5 to 7 minutes. Do not lose that beautiful green color by overcooking! Roll the asparagus in a little unsalted butter to coat.

~~~~

Ingredients
8 egg yolks
8 tablespoons freshly squeezed lemon juice
2 sticks unsalted butter, sliced
Salt

> *White pepper*
> *Tabasco*
> *Dash of cayenne*

Several hours before you are ready to serve, whisk yolks and lemon juice in a cold saucepan. Add sliced butter. Cover the pan and put in the icebox. When ready to serve, remove the saucepan and cook over medium to low heat, whisking all the time. After the sauce has thickened, season to taste with salt, pepper, and Tabasco. Add a dash of cayenne.

Makes two cups.

Sally Lunn

For some reason, men never fail to be impressed by Sally Lunn. Sally Lunn is a kind of bread that developed in England and was popular in the Virginia colony. From there, it spread to Mississippi.

Ingredients
1 package yeast
1 cup whole milk, warmed
3 tablespoons unsalted butter
3 tablespoons sugar
3 large eggs
1 teaspoon vanilla
1 teaspoon salt
3½ cups flour

Preheat the oven to 325°. Allow the yeast to soften in warm milk. Cream butter and sugar. Add the eggs and mix well. Add yeast-milk mixture. Add the vanilla.

Mix the salt with the flour and sift. Sift again.

Add the flour mixture to the butter mixture and beat well. Allow to rise in a warm place until double in size. Beat down again and after a light kneading turn into a well-buttered loaf or bundt pan. Cover and let rise again for an hour or until doubled in size. Bake at 325° for approximately 1 hour or until golden brown.

Serves ten.

Spoon Bread

Spoon bread is another male-impresser. Newlywed or nearly dead, men love it. Therefore we think it's another good dish for a groom candidate of any age.

Spoon bread is baked in a casserole (usually round) and served with a spoon as a side dish. There is not an old-time Southern cookbook that doesn't have at least one recipe for spoon bread.

Ingredients
3 eggs, separated
1 cup boiling water
1 cup sifted cornmeal
1 cup whole milk, scalded
1 teaspoon salt
1/2 teaspoon sugar (optional, but I recommend)
1 teaspoon baking powder
2 tablespoons unsalted butter, melted

Preheat the oven to 350°. Grease a casserole dish with butter. Whip egg whites until soft peaks form. Set aside. Beat yolks. Set aside. Pour boiling water over the cornmeal. Add milk, salt, sugar, baking powder, butter, and egg yolks. Fold in the stiffly beaten egg whites. Pour into the well-buttered dish. Bake at 350° for 45 minutes to 1 hour. Serve immediately. Spoon bread has a tendency to fall, but it is still delicious.

Serves six.

Consommé Rice

This is such standard fare. It's safe (anyone will eat it) and men do love it . . . and that's the point.

~~~~

Ingredients
3 tablespoons butter
1/2 medium onion, chopped
1 1/2 cups rice
1 can (10 1/2 ounces) beef consommé
1 can (10 1/2 ounces) French onion soup
1/2 cup very rich chicken stock
1/2 cup lightly chopped pecans

Preheat the oven to 350°. Melt the butter and sauté the onions.

Add the rice and stir. Add the consommé, French onion soup, and chicken stock.

Transfer to a 2-quart baking dish. Sprinkle with pecans.

Cover tightly and bake at 350° for 45 minutes. Allow to rest, covered, for a few minutes before serving.

Makes eight servings.

Glorified Stuffed Tomatoes

Southerners are obsessed with their tomatoes. Even if the space is not available for a garden, we grow them in pots, bales of hay, anything!

～～～

Ingredients

8 medium tomatoes
1 stick unsalted butter
2 boxes (8 ounces each) fresh mushrooms, sliced
1 cup sour cream
4 teaspoons flour
1 package (4 ounces) crumbled blue cheese
1/2 teaspoon salt
1/4 teaspoon freshly ground pepper
2 tablespoons Dry Sack sherry
1/2 teaspoon Lea & Perrins Worcestershire sauce
Dash of Tabasco
1/4 cup Progresso Italian bread crumbs

Preheat the oven to 375°. Peel the tomatoes and hollow. The easiest way to do this: Immerse the tomatoes in boiling water . . . just until the skin cracks (not more than a minute). Run under cold water to stop the cooking. Slip the point of a paring knife under the skin and the skin will come right off. Use an apple corer and remove the center of the tomato, being careful not to pierce the bottom. Cut ¼ inch off the top and use a pair of kitchen shears to remove the insides (do not discard, this is delicious stuff).

Turn the tomatoes over to drain. A cake rack works perfectly.

Melt butter in a skillet. Add the mushrooms and sauté.

Stir in the sour cream and flour. Continue to cook until hot.

Add blue cheese and stir until blended.

Add salt, pepper, sherry, and Worcestershire sauce. Taste, add Tabasco if needed.

Fill the tomatoes and sprinkle with bread crumbs.

Bake at 375° for 20 minutes or until brown and bubbling.

Serves eight.

Consommé Rice with Almonds

If your daddy doesn't own a pecan grove, here is another version. Southerners have a thing against buying their pecans. They will, however, buy almonds.

~~~~

Ingredients
¼ medium onion, chopped
3 tablespoons butter
1 cup rice
1 can (10½ ounces) beef consommé
1 can (10½ ounces) French onion soup
½ cup slivered almonds

Preheat the oven to 350°.

Saute the onion in melted butter. Add the rice, consommé, and onion soup. Transfer to a 2-quart baking dish, top with almonds, cover tightly, and bake at 350° for 45 minutes. Let rest covered for a few minutes before serving.

Serves eight.

Baked Peaches

These peaches look great as a garnish for the serving platter. We all know that good-looking food tastes better! We've tried using fresh peaches and it just isn't the same. I've used a variety of chutneys, but Major Grey's is the only variety available in most grocery stores in the provinces.

~~~~

Ingredients
1 can freestone peach halves
Unsalted butter
Curry powder
1 bottle of Major Grey's chutney

Preheat the oven to 400°.

Drain the peach halves. Pat dry, if necessary. Place in a baking dish cut side up and brush the peach half with melted butter. Sprinkle lightly with curry powder. Fill the indentation with chutney. Bake at 400° until bubbling hot, about 10 minutes.

Makes six servings.

Bourbon Slush

This is one of those Sunday afternoon drinks that can knock you over in a hurry. Our friend Laurie Gillespie brought these to the lake house. Let's just say that we are more than delighted that her husband is a doctor. After your company leaves, this is a great way to celebrate. Be careful—this is an insidious cocktail that only appeals to females . . . somewhat like aspic. Men would not be caught dead drinking this. But you may need it after entertaining the young man you hope will be the father of your grandchildren.

~~~~

Ingredients
1 small can frozen lemonade
1 small can frozen orange juice
1 tea bag in 2 cups boiling water
6 cups water
2 cups bourbon

Mix all ingredients in a gallon container. Freeze. Stir occasionally. Drink. Easy enough.

Makes one half gallon.

Air Base Cocktail
(Kiss the Boys Good-bye)

This is another one from the late Mrs. Mayhall's repertoire, a tribute to that great institution that helped so many Delta belles avoid the shame of spinsterhood. You may feel *you* can fly after a few.

~~~~

Ingredients
3¼ ounce sloe gin
3¼ ounce brandy
½ an egg white
Juice of 1 lemon

Mix all ingredients and shake with ice. Strain into a cocktail glass.

Makes one strong drink.

FIGS

SOUTHERNERS love to stuff things. We've gotten past the stuffed chicken that spurts juice at you. Stuffed figs, dates, and apricots, however, remain popular.

Slice a small pocket in each fig. Add a tiny ball of gorgonzola or blue cheese.

Wrap with a small piece of bacon (or not). Drizzle with a bit of good olive oil. Bake at 350° on a greased baking sheet until the cheese has melted and the bacon is crisp. Drain carefully.

APRICOTS

SPLIT each dried apricot and add a bit of cream cheese that has been flavored with crystallized ginger. Bleu de Bresse or Boursin can be used in place of the flavored cream cheese.

FIRST DATE

STUFF each seedless date with a piece of pecan, walnut, or almond.

Wrap with a thin slice of bacon and broil on a foil-lined sheet until the bacon is crisp.

Drain on a paper towel.

SECOND DATE

SOAK dates in dry sherry for two days. Proceed with stuffing and broiling.

Dates can also be stuffed with flavored cream cheese. As a change, we like to mix chopped pecans and cream cheese as a stuffing.

Chocolate Roll with Custard

A killer dessert. If this doesn't get him, give up.

CUSTARD

> 1 cup sugar
> 4 eggs, beaten
> 2 tablespoons all-purpose flour
> Pinch of salt
> 3 cups scalded milk
> 1 cup heavy cream
> 1 teaspoon vanilla

CHOCOLATE ROLL

> 3 tablespoons coffee (waste not, want not . . . use your leftover
>   morning coffee)
> 6 ounces dark chocolate (if you live in the provinces, you can use
>   Baker's semisweet chocolate, 6 squares—1 ounce each)
> 6 eggs, separated
> ¾ cup sugar

WHIPPED FILLING

> 1 cup whipping cream, whipped
> ¼ cup confectioners' sugar
> 1 teaspoon vanilla
> Bourbon to taste

Make the custard early in the day. In the top of a double boiler, combine the sugar, beaten eggs, flour, and pinch of salt. Place the mixture over boiling water and slowly add the milk and cream. Stir constantly until the mixture thickens a bit. For this dish, it's better to have a bit thinner custard. Immediately remove the mixture from the heat and add the vanilla. Cover and refrigerate.

Preheat the oven to 375°.

Warm the coffee in a small saucepan. Add the chocolate and continue to stir until the chocolate has melted. Remove from heat.

Meanwhile, whisk the egg yolks and add to the bowl of mixer. Add ¾ cup sugar, a little at a time. Beat well. Add the chocolate mixture to the yolks and incorporate. Beat the egg whites until stiff. Fold into the chocolate/egg mixture.

Grease a 10 × 15 jelly roll pan. Cover the greased pan with waxed paper and grease the waxed paper with unsalted butter. Pour the chocolate mixture onto the waxed paper and smooth.

Bake at 375° for 10 minutes. Leave the pan in the oven, door open, heat off, for 5 more minutes. If the cake begins to brown too much around the edges, remove immediately from the oven. Dampen a dish towel (wring out all excess water), cover the pan with the towel, and invert. Gently peel the waxed paper off the cake.

Flavor the whipped cream with the confectioners' sugar, vanilla, and bourbon to taste.

Spread the cream evenly over the cake . . . saving a bit to garnish each slice.

Starting at one end, roll the cake tightly. Wrap and refrigerate. Allow the cake to chill at least an hour.

When ready to serve, put custard on top of each plate (I prefer a clear plate), top the custard with a slice of cake, top each slice of cake with a dollop of flavored whipped cream, a drizzle of custard, and a few berries A sprig of mint adds a nice touch. To absolutely gild the lily add a chocolate curl or shaving.

Serves eight to ten.

Bride's Biscuits

The bridegroom has been fed like royalty by his mother-in-law to be. After the wedding, he realizes that his new wife doesn't know the first thing about cooking. She needs a recipe to boil water. This is an old recipe that is called Bride's Biscuits because it is easy enough for a newly married lady to "fix."

⟋⟋⟋⟋

Ingredients
½ cup butter, softened
3 ounces cream cheese, softened
1 cup flour

Preheat the oven to 350°.

Mix the butter and cheese until blended. Add the flour and "work" the mixture until a ball of dough forms. Lightly flour a smooth surface and roll the dough. Cut with a small biscuit cutter. Bake at 350° for 10 to 12 minutes or until the biscuits are lightly browned.

Makes at least a dozen biscuits.

FIG PRESERVES

FIG preserves are the Southern version of an aphrodisiac. Also, while the bride is learning to cook, she might like to borrow some of her mother's preserves to dress up her Bride's Biscuits. This recipe comes from Marguerite Shepherd. She is one of the best jelly and preserve makers in Greenville. Marguerite makes everything from scratch, even picking her own fruit. A devoted member of the Thursday beauty parlor club at Hair Tenders, she supplies us with her bounty throughout the year.

You'll need 30 to 35 figs for each jar. Wash figs and remove the stems. Drain well. Put figs in a Dutch oven and cover with sugar. Refrigerate overnight with the lid on. Bring to a boil (without lid) and reduce heat to low/medium. Cook for about 20 minutes, or until clear and glazed-like. With a slotted spoon, remove the figs and let them drain well. Using the smallest amount of juice possible, fill heated, sterilized jars with the figs. Cook juice 10 to 15 minutes longer. Pour juice over figs and seal. All the juice will not be used—but save it! It's delicious used as fig syrup.

Marguerite puts her jars, without the lids, on a cookie sheet and heats them in the oven.

continued

She uses a funnel to pour the juice into the jars, which keeps the jars from getting sticky and makes for a perfect seal.

You can do pears the same way. Marguerite likes the old-timey heavy "Club Aluminum" when cooking the pears. It produces beautiful, rich, golden preserves.

Grandmama Milly's Tomato Aspic

What not to serve: Men never care for aspic. But ladies love it, and, as daughters of the South, we simply must include at least one aspic recipe. This recipe is from our friend Lucy Shackelford, who inherited it from her grandmother Mildred Lacey. It is so delicious that you might even get raves from men. It is more highly seasoned than most aspics and uses V8 juice instead of tomato juice.

The secret of this aspic is that it is made to taste like a good Bloody Mary. Lucy admits to having used Major Peters Bloody Mary Mix several times, at the request of her father-in-law, Duke Shackelford.

~~~~

Ingredients
3 cups V8 juice (divided use)
⅓ cup lemon juice (do NOT used processed kind)
2 tablespoons Lea & Perrins Worcestershire sauce
Dash Tabasco
2 tablespoons unflavored gelatin
1 package (8 ounces) cream cheese (do NOT use low-fat cream cheese)
Salt and pepper to taste

Bring 2½ cups V8 to a boil, along with lemon juice, Lea & Perrins, and Tabasco. Soak unflavored gelatin in remaining

½ cup V8 juice and dissolve thoroughly into hot mixture. Mix 1 cup of hot mixture with the cream cheese until smooth. Pour cream cheese mixture into the bottom of 8 to 12 individual ramekins/molds (depending on size—about 1 to 1½ inches thick) or pour the whole thing into a 6- to 8-cup mold (if using one larger mold, double V8 portion of this recipe—do not double cream cheese part). Be sure to grease the mold well with vegetable oil, olive oil, or mayonnaise. Let this layer, which will be the top layer, set up in the fridge until fairly firm. When firm, pour remaining juice mixture over and place in fridge to finish congealing.

Optional ingredients to add to tomato layer include olives, chopped celery, lump crabmeat, boiled shrimp, etc.

To serve, unmold and sprinkle with some good Hungarian paprika and perhaps a few capers. Serve with homemade mayonnaise. Please do not use sto-bought mayonnaise!

Serves ten.

3

~~~~

The Pageant: Are You Trying to Marry Off Your Daughter or Win the Academy Award for Bad Taste?

ALTHOUGH MR. AND MRS. Marston Moore IV have become grandparents many times over, their wedding is still considered the gold standard for perfection in the Mississippi Delta. A country wedding in the bride's yard, amid flickering hurricane lamps, it is remembered with particular admiration by Greenville's old ladies, who are charged with the task of ensuring that civilization continues. What was special about this wedding? Not the huge wedding party—Mrs. Moore was attended by several cousins, her roommate from Sophie Newcomb, and a handful of friends she'd known all her life. There was no fondue fountain spouting chocolate liqueur. While the trellised wedding cake—topped with still-living flowers—was certainly lovely, there were no sugar-spun bridges connecting it to satellite cakes.

What makes this wedding loom large in the annals of Delta

nuptials: the absolutely flawless magnolias carried by the bride and bridesmaids, whose ecru gowns the blossoms perfectly matched. The magnolias had been plucked from the bough— which was in the front yard, of course—at the exact moment they attained the precise degree of beige required to comple- ment the attendants' gowns. A magnolia is easily bruised, and its glory is measured in hours. Yet a force greater than nature—the bride's mother—had seen to it that these magnolias would be at their apogee for the march up the aisle. No doubt somebody stood by with the garden shears while the bridal party dressed. It is almost certain that these ephemerals perished before the last glass of champagne was drunk.

Sprays of faultless flowers would hardly catapult a Delta wed- ding to legend status today. It would take umpteen bridesmaids, blaring trumpets in the church, and a multitude of parties given by host committees rather than friends, not to mention a string of vulgar limousines, to gain a toehold in fame. As true daugh- ters of the great Southland, we are second to none in appreciat- ing big blowouts, and would curl up and die before saying weddings have gotten too big. Is there such a thing as a party that's *too* big? Nuptial blowouts are part of our heritage. Still, we can't help noticing that weddings are evolving into spectacles ri- valing our beloved Miss America pageant—except not always as meaningful. "What's wrong with cheese straws, nuts, mints, and finger sandwiches?" asks an old-fashioned wedding guru who is growing jaded in the face of let's-go-to-the-poorhouse-tomorrow reception fare.

Why have weddings turned into extravaganzas? Because they

are no longer life-changing events—that's why. With the love-birds often already chirping at the same return address, it is the pageant itself that must create the drama of that still special, but not quite *sooooo* special as it once was, day. Forget mere etiquette—to wed properly today, the participants must pretend they're in a reality show. We can't help but recall the bride whose affections were captured by a local policeman. Harking back to the sixties, their wedding had a pig theme. They served pigs in a blanket, and the groom's cake was a police car created entirely from do-nut holes (a reminder of the groom's beloved 7-Eleven convenience store, where pillars of local law enforcement hang out eating doughnuts between bouts with the forces of evil). Oh, and did we mention that the bride and groom sat on horses? Unfortunately, horseback nuptials aren't as rare as one might wish. Our mothers would call this vulgar! Alas, the old vulgar is the new everybody's-doing-it.

The lead-up to the pageant—we mean wedding—begins immediately after a ring has been slipped onto the young lady's finger. The engagement was once a pleasant, somewhat hectic, interlude when the bride-to-be was entertained by her friends and family. Now she is entertained by everybody she has ever laid her eyes on. A friend of the bride's mother becomes the party coordinator, and would-be hostesses have to work through her to be listed as one of the forty-nine hostesses for an intimate luncheon for a bride they've hardly said boo to. In the past, it was enough that the bride and her mother were pleased and grateful to their hostesses—today, bridal luncheon invitations have so many names that they read like benefit committees. Showers, once rare in the Delta, where genteel teas reigned, have made inroads, not always in the most dignified manner. Would you believe LeCarol Bentley, a Baptist from a small town that shall remain anonymous, was feted with a lingerie shower in the vacation Bible schoolroom? One good thing we can say for the Baptists, though: They don't go in for bar-stocking showers, which can get, as we say down here, right expensive.

The bride has always made her entrance on the arm of her father or the male relative deputed to do the honors—but now all too often, doors of the church vestibule must be flung open to blaring trumpets that seem to shout, "Here I Am, Look at Me." In the past, no belle of the old Southland felt she had to shout, "Look at Me"—she knew that you were looking at her. It was her birthright. Today, she has to compete for attention with a printed program that rolls the credits—we mean lists the names—of the wedding party, with their cities of origin, and is all too frequently adorned with cooing turtledoves. Remember when we used to actually know the entire wedding party? Oh, well—the programs do make good fans.

Delta heat is, of course, historically an unavoidable feature of all summer weddings, large or small, proper or improper, a fact of life that *Martha Stewart Living* brides rarely need take into consideration. Heat is just the sort of thing that the bride in a small Southern town (again, we grant anonymity) might have wanted to factor in before she hit upon the idea of a medieval-themed wedding. (In the past, "we're getting married" was the theme of all weddings.) Lining the walkway into the church, the grooms-men glowed (which is Delta for "sweated bullets") in their full suits of armor. Pelts of a too realistic nature hung on their shields. Historians tell us that the Middle Ages were a pungent time in mankind's history, and so was this wedding. Even if the air-conditioning had functioned properly, which it did not (air-conditioning traditionally goes out at weddings), no amount of Old Spice could have made the groomsmen pleasing in an olfactory sense. We were definitely ready to quaff some mead when we got to the country club.

Hot weather, unlike bad taste, is inescapable in our neck of the woods. We'll never forget the wedding—a very nice wedding—at which the brother of the bride, affected by a combination of the July inferno and malfunctioning air-conditioning, began wobbling and weaving at the front of the church. Soon he lurched forward, clutching at a hurricane lamp (we love candles in hot weather!), which, fortunately, another groomsman caught, thereby preventing the proceedings from getting even hotter. The unconscious brother was dragged unceremoniously from the church by the loyal groomsmen. The couple then knelt to repeat their vows. Unfortunately, the minister had words of wisdom to offer—and offer, and offer. He preached so long that there was an audible stirring in the pews, and then he launched into an equally lengthy address to the Almighty. Finally, the bride rose. "Ah'm not finished," the minister said, sotto voce. "Ah am," said the bride. "Ah'm 'bout to pass out. Ah have to stand up." The couple was saying their vows *a pied* when brother, semi-revived but still glassy-eyed, appeared with a glass of ice water for his sister. The soloist, a soprano, simply shut her eyes and started singing the Lord's Prayer. She didn't stop until she sensed that the last attendant was safely down the aisle. Members of the wedding party were met in the vestibule by doctors dispensing ice-cold Co-Colas (Deltese for Coca-Cola).

Accidents of weather were not what made another big wedding memorable—it was bad taste, pure and simple. If you can have bad taste for free, go for it. But this wasn't free, and we got the distinct feeling that the family wanted to impress upon us how not-for-free it was. We love tents in the yard (nice people don't say lawn), champagne, and white gardenias. We are less enthusiastic about Fostoria crystal votive candle holders, twinkling electric "stars," and twenty-foot mirrors and stained-glass windows inside the tent where the ceremony takes place. Not to mention the three life-sized cherubs from the 1984 World's Fair holding Victorian floral arrangements. The father of the bride bragged to the local newspaper that he was putting on such a theatrical wedding to help promote his town. And we thought he was just trying to give his daughter a nice send-off. The cateress did not improve matters by telling the newspaper that caviar had been "shipped from New York" (like we thought it was grown on Bubba Billson's catfish farm?) and that the whole affair was "top-of-the-line."

When the redoubtable Mrs. Crump presided over social coverage, such a quote would never have made it into print. Yes, wedding write-ups have changed, too. It used to be that newspaper announcements, both for the engagement and the wedding itself, followed a formal structure, shunning middle initials for full names. The essential data, including names of the couple's grandparents, was given, and perhaps a few nice details about the bride's dress or the refreshments. It was also customary to tell who "poured" and who greeted at the front door. The format was for the most part standard, and families knew what to expect. We remember the grandmother who cheerfully paid a semester's tuition for her granddaughter, who was not college material at all. The granddaughter lasted all of a week. Nevertheless the grandmother was pleased with her investment. "It was worth it," she explained, "because now, when Sistuh marries, the announcement will say, 'She attended Mississippi State College for Women.'"

Announcements nowadays will say almost anything the couple is crazy enough to want to share with all mankind. Did we really need to know that Miss Lottie May Lowman "wore a petite size 2 designer gown from Paris"? Was our morning coffee improved by the sight of a grinning groom, barefooted and wearing "tuxedo" shorts? No. We most certainly concur with the bride who said, "But, Mrs. Jones, *everyone* is entitled to *one* white wedding." Indeed, we assert that there is such a thing as too much candor. A wedding announcement that begins, "Billy Wayne Garrett, 5, is pleased to announce the impending nuptials of his parents, Nelda Jean Akers and Billy Wayne Senior," has already said too much. We feel certain Mrs. Crump would have crumpled this in a white-gloved hand.

Speaking of Miss Lottie May's aforementioned petite size 2, one thing never changes: the bride's determination to have a nineteen-inch waist on her special day. When a bride-to-be steps onto a box to have to have her dress fitted, look out! Stand back with smelling salts and ice water: She is fixin' to faint. You would, too, if you hadn't eaten in three days. For many brides, being pencil-thin is as important, if not more so, than being in love. The daunting prospect of a size 10 is cause to elope. The perfect look for the stylish Delta lady, by the way, bridal or otherwise, also features a tan, attainable inside the sorority houses of Ole Miss, where sunlamps are more popular than actually venturing out of doors (where you might be attacked by vicious mosquitoes). If you can become wraithlike by subsisting for weeks on end on nothing but Diet Co-Colas, and look as if somebody has poured a can of shellac on you, don't change a thing. You have attained perfection.

A Tennessee family we know felt that it wasn't enough for the bride to attain perfection. They wanted the whole family to look like the Olsen twins. Unfortunately, they had cultivated the unbecoming *Super Size Me* look. The solution: gastric bypass surgery. For the bride, the groom, and both sets of parents. We kid you not. During the wedding, a creaking sound, not unlike bursting water pipes, was heard. The congregation froze (not unlike water pipes). Could it be that all that expensive gastric surgery was coming undone at the worst time imaginable? Thank heavens it soon became apparent what really was happening: Twin movie screens were being rolled down above the altar for—what else?—biographical videos. But not *too* biographical. We couldn't help but notice that all the pictures were post-bypass.

Greenville brides of a certain age (and never mind what that age might be) will tell you that a wedding dress from Mrs. L. A. White was well worth the trouble—to starve for, you might say. Mrs. L. A. White was called La White by Tout Greenville—

which some of us pronounce Toot Greenville. La White's shop was in a Victorian house (ne-vuh say mansion—that's tacky and pretentious, and we always tell our children that when you're being tacky and pretentious, try not to be obvious about it) downtown off Washington Avenue, the main drag, which then had a bou-le-vard down the middle. La White's aplomb was the stuff of legend. When a nervous bride spilled bright pink punch down her front just as the initial strains of "O Perfect Love" were wafting through the hot, sultry air, La White was the picture of sangfroid (we're on a French binge). "My dear, calm down," she said to the bride. "Just stand still for a minute." La White dabbed and pinned for a few seconds, and order was restored to the universe. "You would never have known," recalled a bridesmaid, still awed after many years. (Maybe the moral of this story is: If you're going to drink on your wedding day, stick to gin?) Unfortunately, La White didn't "do" all Delta weddings. We know one she should have—the bridesmaids carried bouquets of flowers with upright, wiggling pistils. Stifled giggles could be heard, especially when the soloist launched into "Fount of All Blessings."

Although La White is but a fond memory, Delta brides still enjoy nonpareil shopping opportunities (this is the last *mot français*—we promise). It should come as no surprise that one of the country's largest vendors of (small, we hope) wedding dresses is nearby in Brinkley, Arkansas. It is Low's Bridal and Formal Shoppe, owned by Dorcas Prince, whose mother founded the enterprise by selling a few wedding dresses in her husband's pharmacy. A girl can bring her grandmother's Belgian lace veil, and Dorcas will find a dress that goes with it. Dorcas has also matched turquoise cowboy boots for a less traditional ensemble. Mrs. Prince says the shop has flourished "by the grace of God and a fluke of nature," which is probably just the way Fifth Avenue merchants talk. A historical note: In the 1920s and '30s, a "Doctor" Brinkley attained national fame through his experiments with goat glands. He dreamed of Viagra before its time, or, as a radio ditty put it, the goat glands were supposed to "make a man the ram what am with every lamb." Many believe that Brinkley was named in honor of the doctor, and that Dorcas's ancestral pharmacy was associated with the experiments. We regret to report that neither of these rumors is true, though the great state of Arkansas did give the good doc something all other states denied him: a medical license.

At any rate, Low's has since moved from the humble pharmacy into an elegantly refurbished old railroad hotel with chandeliers and a selection of gowns that get more expensive as you go to the next floor. Budget-conscious brides should stay away from the stairs! According to *Southern Living* magazine, there are more wedding gowns at Low's than there are citizens of Brinkley (population: 4,000). You can easily drive to Brinkley from Greenville, but real big shots love flying in big-shot style—never mind that the metropolitan aeronautical facility is for crop dusters. "I flew in like Barney Fife," said a rattled shopper from Atlanta. But she did get to ride into town in Brinkley's elegant "courtesy car." It is a former po-lice vehicle, and it takes you directly to Low's, there not being a whole heck of a lot of other major attractions in Brinkley.

It has been remarked that people in the Delta frequently look better in their obituary write-ups than they did in life; unfortunately, they often look worse in their wedding clippings—and it's their own fault. Any living being should know that if you're the groom, you don't wear sunglasses for your photo op. (Of course, we understood the impulse to be incognito: The new missus sported an ever-so-subtle mustache.) She was quite unlike the perfectionist bride who stamped her dainty foot and flatly refused to set it inside the church until Rhonda from Hair Tenders returned to respray an errant curl. (A lady from the wedding guild crawled on all fours to tell the organist, who was in his fifth rendition of Trumpet Voluntary, to keep going— Rhonda was on the way. Then the wedding guild lady had to crawl out of the sanctuary.) There is the category of clippings that deserves the headline: "Let's Put Something Funny on Our Heads and Get Married." This is not an innovation. Some of our grandmothers wore things on their heads that made them look ridiculous at this pivotal moment in life. Old Mrs. Jeffrey wore something that looked like a papal tiara at her sacred moment, while her sister Annie Jane bore an unfortunate resemblance to Theodora of Byzantium when she married that good-for-nothing Buddy Boy James. At the opposite end of the spectrum, one hapless bride was persuaded to don a bridal cap, which was touted as the epitome of simple chic. This young lady came into the church looking like a dead ringer for Esther Williams. Well, she *was* on the swim team. Note to flapper-inspired brides: A twenties-style fillet around your head doesn't go well with a bouffant the size of a loaf of Wonder Bread.

While the reception has become more of an extravaganza, too many families now dispense with the simple nicety of a receiving line. Even small receptions at home require a receiving line. If the family was detained at the church to take pictures (a good time to take pictures: *after*, not during, the ceremony), the bride's mother's best friends, known as floating hostesses, receive until the family arrives. The bride and groom are first in line and the assumption, if she was marrying a foreigner from someplace like New York, is that the groom's family might not know everybody. It is customary to shake hands with a guest who is then presented to the next person in the receiving line. The bride's mother might turn to the person next to her and say, "This is Ardella Dell Rogers, and we went to the W. together." The father of the bride circulates; he is charged with making sure everyone has a drink, funny because the one thing all Southerners can hone in on is the bar, an early form of GPS.

All our mothers have funny receiving line stories—such as the time the town wag went down a receiving line smiling profusely and uttering things like, "Your mother is the meanest old biddy in Greenville . . . That hat must have come from the attic . . . You must be awfully glad Uncle Henry finally croaked and left you the farm." Not a soul noticed—or, if they did, they were too polite to let on. One elderly lady's name was mangled into a word you probably wouldn't hear in a bordello, much less the Greenville Country Club—it was filthy, but it made it all the way down the line. We doubt if the little old lady even knew what it meant. But we did. You could follow the stunned faces down the receiving line. Whatever abuses there may have been in the past, we feel that not having a receiving line is a contemporary form of wedding abuse. There's no harm in being introduced once again to your vague aunt who asks sweetly, "Don't I know you?"

One tradition that has been admirably upheld is the rehearsal party, which is eagerly awaited and traditionally hosted by the groom's family. In the South, this is a sit-down dinner party. "If you didn't have a rehearsal, when would you get drunk?" puzzles one Delta belle who will no doubt find her way to Greenville's popular AA hut sooner rather than later. The bride, however, tries not to drink as much as she usually does—no bride wants puffy eyes on her special day. The rehearsal dinner is a test of willpower for the Delta bride; good thing the MOB watches her like a hawk.

Another beloved tradition is having a proxy for the bride during the rehearsal at church, perhaps, in an era when brides do not await the wedding night with curiosity, a quaint custom. But we like it. "The best weddings are the ones where the bride and groom don't already live together. They are special," says a Delta wedding guild lady. The second best are when the bride will shriek and carry on as if she's never even been farther than Itta Bena unchaperoned. A little hypocrisy (aka, the tribute vice pays to virtue) here is not always a bad thing. Some of the greatest Delta loose legs have been amenable to re-virgination, if only for a fleeting evening. We say: Keep the proxy! And it gives the MOB another line in the program.

While we do unabashedly call for a teensy weensy bit of hypocrisy, we think that the best advice for a successful wedding is: Be yourself. A wedding offers an opportunity to be somebody you aren't. This is a temptation to be (for the most part) resisted. If you can afford a big blowout, by all means, do it. But if you can't afford a band from Memphis, a small wedding reception in the living room with mints and nuts is just as lovely. One of the Delta's most famous families, the Minor Millsaps, specializes in small, at-home weddings. "I don't know anybody who's ever been to a Millsaps wedding," said one of the best friends of one of the Millsaps girls. A good rule of thumb: Don't spend more time planning the wedding than the marriage is expected to last. Of course, moderation in all things is desirable. It is possible to be *too* yourself. In this unlovely category we put the joining of Ethel and Charlie, whose last names we graciously withhold. Charlie is a plumbing contractor, and punch was served at the Ramada Inn reception from "porcelain receptacles." The newspaper described it as "a party never to be forgotten." But we are trying to—er—flush the memory from our consciousness.

Still, wretched excesses aside, the best moments at weddings are always the most genuine moments. When Iris Rosenberg was married in her backyard, the family's elderly cocker spaniel, Brandy, fell into the swimming pool. Iris's father, a local department store owner, jumped, tux and all, into the pool to rescue the much-loved pet. It was a lovely wedding to start with, but the rescue is what made it even more memorable. Love, you see, is what matters most in making a wedding a success.

We have nothing against the big wedding, as we said—if you can afford it and if it's you. One of the all-time greatest of the big Delta weddings took place out from, as we like to say,

Greenwood, Mississippi. It was an evening wedding with groomsmen in tails (we know we don't have to tell *you* that tails are worn only in the evening!) and tents big enough for the Ringling Bros. Circus. Since the reception was about eighteen miles from town, men were hired to direct traffic down a winding dirt road. A pharmaceuticals salesman from Detroit made the wrong turn and got in the line and ended up at the reception. "Where am I?" he asked as his car door was opened by a valet. "At tha weddin'," came the reply. The salesman had a dandy time and made so many new friends that he requested a transfer to Mississippi. Speaking of getting lost—we can't imagine why—it's always a good idea to have hired cars for the bridal party. One groomsman reminisced, "I don't recall how I got back to Greenwood. But I must have, because here I am."

A far less elaborate affair, however, was also a perfect wedding. It took place when our famous air base was still in business. The late Bern Keating, a Greenville photographer and travel writer, happened into a church—we don't know how— that wasn't Bern's usual stomping ground. But never mind. A young girl from New Jersey was standing alone in the vestibule, waiting to go up the aisle to marry her cadet. "Who's going to walk you up the aisle?" Bern asked. She explained that, because of wartime austerities, even her mother, her only living parent, could not make it. Whereupon Bern offered his arm. When the minister asked who was giving this woman in holy matrimony Bern replied, "Her mother and I." It doesn't get any better than that—and it also goes to show you that a girl from New Jersey can have a perfect Delta wedding, if she's lucky.

LINDA'S FAMOUS REHEARSAL
DINNERS

Wᴇ cannot discuss rehearsal dinners in the Delta without mentioning the late Linda Haik. Linda—everybody called her Linda—was the best caterer of her day—and her day was one of graciousness. When the movie *Baby Doll* was shot in Benoit, Mississippi, we were thrilled for two reasons—first because the movie was "banned by the Vatican," which was very exciting, and second because all those deprived actors got a taste of Delta cuisine at its best, prepared by Linda.

Linda catered for our mothers and grandmothers and a few of us who were lucky enough to get married while Linda still reigned supreme. A stalwart of St. James' Episcopal Church, Linda, a small dynamo of Lebanese descent, had such long histories with so many Greenville families that we sometimes wondered if she gave a Shabby Genteel Discount for families down on their luck. Linda introduced Greenville to tenderloin, which used to require a trip to Memphis, and revealed the secret of cooking with potatoes: Use those big, ordinary potatoes, and not the little red new potatoes you think are so hotsy totsy. The big ones have a better flavor.

continued

A typical Linda cocktail party might have a ham at one end and a turkey at the other, with a hot seafood dip in a chafing dish and Linda's famous marinated tomatoes and avocados (see "Restorative Cocktail," page 225) somewhere in between. This arrangement also worked well for parties to announce engagements. One of Linda's last big parties was a wedding supper buffet for our dear friend Roberta Shaw, truly one of the greatest of all last Delta weddings. But it was of the old-fashioned kind—that is, there were just old friends rather than a creative director. "It all started with the 'rehearsal dinner' at Doe's [our favorite restaurant]," Roberta recalled. "I think we were rehearsing for some really serious drinking later that night." We seem to remember going to a cottage on nearby Lake Ferguson, for more imbibing. The wedding was in Roberta's living room. Linda served her famous Oysters Rockefeller on the long, formal dinning table. Through the blur, we seem to recall Billy Nearing with his hand *in* the chafing dish, as he chatted up out-of-town visitors. We think he may have been tipsy, because he was later spotted dancing naked in his parents' driveway. We are glad to say that his burns were minor.

Oysters Rockefeller

In Louisiana, people are wont to ask, "How you like dem ersters?" At Lillo's, a popular Leland restaurant that has fed the Delta for generations, they're on the menu as Oysters Rockafella. Sounds like a dance. We don't have Linda's recipe, but this one is delicious and offered in her memory. These oysters will make you rocka, fella!

~~~~

Ingredients

2 pints oysters or 4 dozen small fresh oysters, shucked

3 sticks unsalted butter

4 bunches green onions, chopped (3/4 cup)

4 packages (10 ounces each) frozen chopped spinach, cooked and drained

3 cloves garlic, pressed

1/2 cup parsley, chopped

3/4 cup celery, minced

1 teaspoon thyme

1 teaspoon marjoram

1 teaspoon basil

1/2 teaspoon cayenne

3 tablespoons Lea & Perrins Worcestershire sauce

2 tablespoons Tabasco

1 tablespoon lemon juice

3/4 tablespoon anchovy paste

> 2 to 3 tablespoons Pernod, or ½ teaspoon ground anise seed
> ½ cup freshly grated Parmesan cheese
> 1 cup seasoned bread crumbs

Preheat oven to 375°.

Drain the oysters and save the juice. Pat them dry. If you use oysters that have just been shucked, drain in a colander (save the juice) and pat them dry. Layer oysters in a shallow dish. Bake at 375° 5 to 10 minutes, or until the edges just begin to curl. Chop the oysters and save until the sauce is ready.

In a large skillet, melt the butter and sauté the onions, celery, and garlic. Add the spinach and parsley. Stir. Remove from the heat and add remaining ingredients with the exception of oysters, Parmesan cheese, and bread crumbs. In a food processor, puree the greens and seasonings. Return to a Dutch oven and cook over low heat for about 30 minutes. If the sauce gets too thick, thin with a bit of the reserved oyster juice.

Add the oysters and cook about 30 more minutes. Stir in the Parmesan cheese and bread crumbs. Transfer to a chafing dish. Serve with toast points or small rounds of French bread. The sauce is so good that sometimes people don't even add the oysters.

THE REHEARSAL DINNER

A REHEARSAL party should reflect the groom. It's his—or his mother's—moment to shine. In many instances, the groom is from out of town, and this is his family's introduction to the bride's community. With so many people meeting each other for the first time, it's a good idea to work conversational gambits into the planning. When Gayden's nephew, who lives in Alabama, married a Jackson, Mississippi, girl, the rehearsal dinner was held in the Mississippi Museum of Art in Jackson. Gayden toted every piece of McCarty pottery she owned to Jackson. Pup and Lee McCarty are Mississippi's premier potters, but the distinctive pottery served a less obvious function than holding cheese straws—something to talk about. There was a band during cocktails for the same reason—the noise eased tension.

Sometimes random seating is fine—but not at a party with lots of people who don't know everybody. Place cards are essential then. In addition to place cards, to the side of everyone's napkin was a card with the evening's cast of characters: "Anne Call, Grandmother of the Groom." A close friend or relative was also assigned to serve as host at every table. After dinner, the band struck up again, and we had a table of after-dinner drinks before

continued

saying good night. We didn't want an abrupt ending to such a nice night. Gayden put together an inexpensive goodie bag of aspirin, Alka-Seltzer, and mints, plus note-cards with helpful Jackson telephone numbers, such as for taxis, a pharmacist, or an attorney. Billy Nearing was away at the time, so maybe nobody really needed a lawyer. But it helped give guests yet another conversation starter.

Sausage Cheese Balls

Since the groom's mother, Marsue Dean Lancaster, presides over her family's third-generation sausage business in Gadsden, Alabama, sausage was an appropriate item on the menu. But these are delicious even if you are in another line of endeavor. They were small (you know we're obsessed with little everythings!) and served at the bar . . . lots better than peanuts! A good rule: There should always be something to munch on at the bar.

~~~~

Ingredients
1 pound Dean *sausage, hot, not mild
3½ cups Bisquick
10 ounces extra-sharp cheese

Preheat the oven to 375°.

Crumble sausage with Bisquick. Melt cheese in double boiler. Add to sausage and Bisquick mix. Work with hands until thoroughly mixed. Shape into small balls. Place on a baking sheet about ½ inch apart. Bake at 375° until lightly browned, about 15 or 20 minutes.

Makes about seventy-five balls.

*Note: Marsue's factory is *not* Jimmy Dean—she calls herself "the other Dean."

More Sausage Cheese Balls

We just couldn't stop ourselves with that sausage theme! We're such pigs. This is a quick and easy recipe, a good one for a lazy person.

~~~~

Ingredients
8 ounces extra-sharp cheese, shredded
1 pound sausage
2 cups Bisquick
Tabasco to taste

Preheat the oven to 400°.

Mix ingredients. Shape into small balls and bake at 400° until brown.

These freeze well.

Makes about fifty balls.

Shrimp Remoulade

One of the best cookbooks ever is *The Plantation Cookbook* from The Junior League of New Orleans. Their recipe for shrimp remoulade sauce is simply the best. Use a parfait glass to create an original presentation for this tried and true dish. Make the sauce in a Cuisinart. A note of caution: Do not use absurdly large shrimp. They are hard to eat and often tough. For this recipe, you'll need three pounds of boiled, peeled, de-veined shrimp. This is an excellent first course for a seated dinner.

~~~~

Ingredients
1 head pretty lettuce (anything other than iceberg)
½ cup minced onions
¾ cup oil
¼ cup tarragon vinegar
½ cup country Dijon mustard or brown Creole mustard
2 teaspoons paprika
1 teaspoon cayenne pepper
2 teaspoons salt
2 cloves garlic, pressed
½ cup chopped green onions

Process all ingredients, except lettuce, just long enough to blend. I would suggest the pulse mode. You *do not* want a puree. Chill the sauce overnight.

Put a layer of lettuce, a few shrimp, and some chilled sauce in the parfait glass. Continue the layering process until you reach the top of the glass. You should end with the remoulade sauce on top.

Serves eight.

Quail with Madeira

We would not suggest that you attempt to hunt your rehearsal dinner fare. There are farms that raise and supply a lovely product. The only time we've seen anybody refuse a quail was when our friend Gladys Whitney was served one with two poached quail eggs on top. She burst into tears and said, "I just can't eat the entire family." Her luncheon partner had no such reservations.

Ingredients
8 boned or semi-boned quail
Salt and pepper
Flour
2 sticks unsalted butter
3 ribs celery
Sliced lemons

1 cup Madeira
1 cup consommé
2 bay leaves
Thyme

Preheat the oven to 350°.

Wash and dry the quail. Rub each quail with salt and pepper. Lightly flour each quail. Melt 3 tablespoons of butter in a skillet (black iron skillet preferred). Sauté the quail in batches until brown. If the butter begins to burn, wipe out the skillet and start anew with fresh butter. Place the birds in a baking dish. Cut a rib of celery to fit under each bird (about a three-inch piece for each bird). Place 2 lemon slices on top of each bird. Pour the Madeira and consommé into the sauté pan. Add the bay leaves and a sprinkling of thyme. Bring to a boil. Pour this mixture over the birds. Cover and bake at 350° for 1 hour or until tender.

Serves eight.

Stuffed Tomatoes

Remember the scene in *Steel Magnolias* when Shirley MacLaine says she raises tomatoes because she is an old Southern lady and old Southern ladies raise tomatoes? Southerners are obsessed with their tomatoes.

Tomatoes are an everyday dish, but this isn't an everyday presentation. What makes these tomatoes so spectacular is the curried mayonnaise. You may find yourself eating it with a spoon. Not good for the prenuptial waistline. Get your digestives ready.

~~~~

Ingredients
6 large tomatoes, peeled
Salt and pepper
Dill weed
1 pint mushrooms, sliced
2 jars (6 ounces each) marinated artichoke hearts, drained
A good vinaigrette (what we used to call oil and vinegar)
2 bunches asparagus, peeled, lightly steamed, and chilled

CURRIED MAYONNAISE

1 cup sour cream
2 cups homemade mayonnaise
4 teaspoons curry powder

3 teaspoons lemon juice
2 heaping teaspoons grated onion

Slice about ¼ inch from the top of each tomato. Hollow the tomato, being careful not to pierce the bottom. Save the innards. Turn the tomatoes over to drain. When dry, lightly salt and pepper the insides, add a sprinkle of dill weed, cover, and refrigerate. Marinate the mushrooms and artichoke hearts in the vinaigrette.

Before assembling, drain the mushroom/artichoke mixture well. Cut the heart in halves or thirds. Fill each tomato with the mushrooms and artichokes. Top with the curried mayonnaise. Trim the asparagus so that two spears will fit into the top of each tomato, a decorative touch. You can use the leftover stems for soup. (What an impression the Depression had on our parents!) To make the mayonnaise, blend ingredients until well-incorporated and refrigerate overnight, if possible. It's even better the second day.

Serves six.

Wild Rice and Tomato Tartlets

Perfect, if you're featuring any game.

⌐⌐⌐⌐

Ingredients

16 mini tart shells, partially cooked
1 box (6 ounces) long grain and wild rice, cooked
3 cloves of garlic, minced
2 tablespoons oil
1 can (16 ounces) Progresso Italian tomatoes with basil, drained
  and chopped
1 bar (8 ounces) cream cheese, softened
1 teaspoon salt
1 teaspoon freshly ground pepper
1 teaspoon Lea & Perrins Worcestershire sauce
2 teaspoons Tabasco
½ teaspoon lemon juice
4 eggs, well beaten

Make your own tart shells, if time permits. But know you can buy them. Either way, be sure to glaze the partially cooked shells before filling.

Preheat the oven to 375°.

An egg beaten with 1 tablespoon of water will provide the perfect glaze.

Use a small brush and cover the inside of each shell with the above mixture. Bake the shells at 375° for about 2 or 3 minutes.

In a large skillet, heat the oil and brown the garlic. Add the drained tomatoes, rice, and seasonings. Add the cream cheese and stir until melted. Add beaten eggs and combine well.

Taste to check seasoning.

Fill each shell a little over half full. Bake at 375° for about 15 minutes or until brown and bubbly. This will also fill one 10-inch pie shell if you prefer.

Serves sixteen with mini shells or six to eight if using a pie shell.

Jane Dubberly's Catfish Pate

Jane Dubberly and her husband are both great cooks. They are in the spice business, so you know this is going to be a treat.

~~~~

Ingredients

2 quarts water
1/4 cup Zatarain's liquid crab boil
2 pounds catfish filets
2 envelopes Knox unflavored gelatin
1/2 cup cold water
1 carton (8 ounces) sour cream
1 package (8 ounces) cream cheese
1 can (10¾ ounces) cream of mushroom soup
3 eggs (chicken eggs!), hard-boiled, chopped
1 cup green onion, chopped fine
¾ cup celery, chopped fine
1/2 cup green bell pepper, chopped fine
1/2 cup pimiento, chopped
1 tablespoon lemon juice
1 tablespoon Lea & Perrins Worcestershire sauce
Morton's Nature's Seasonings, to taste
Tabasco, to taste

Boil 2 quarts water with crab boil, add fish to boiling water, and reduce heat and cook 8 to 10 minutes.

Drain and flake fish.

Combine gelatin with ½ cup cold water, and let stand 5 minutes. Dissolve over hot water.

In a mixing bowl combine sour cream, cream cheese, and soup. Blend until smooth, add gelatin, and blend. Fold in fish, eggs, onion, celery, green pepper, pimiento, lemon juice, Worcestershire sauce, Morton's Nature's Seasonings, and Tabasco. Pour mixture into a 1½-quart mold and chill. Serve on Bremmer crackers—or with hard-boiled quail eggs.

This recipe makes enough for 50 servings.

QUAIL EGGS WITH PATE

W E regard quail eggs as the height of elegance. Who doesn't? They are served hard-boiled and peeled (not easy, but your daughter is only going to marry once—we hope). Split the eggs and put a dollop of catfish pate on each half.

As we've said already, sometimes the secret to a good cook is knowing the right numbers to call. Here are two relevant numbers, one for quail eggs and another for a delicious variety of catfish pate:

Strickland Quail Farm
Pooler, Georgia
(912) 748-5769

Taste of Gourmet (for catfish pate)
Indianola, Mississippi
(662) 887-2522

Green Bean and Roquefort Salad

This was served at an outdoor casual wedding party in Arkansas. Because the hosts live out in the country, they always have a well-stocked pantry and a vegetable garden. You have to drive miles to any restaurant, so there is a lot of entertaining at home. This salad was served with grilled tenderloin, sliced tomatoes, and peppered fresh peaches.

Cook the beans the day before.

Ingredients
3 pounds fresh green beans
1 ham hock
1 onion, quartered
1 clove garlic, halved
Salt
Freshly ground pepper
Lawry's seasoning salt

Cover green beans with water and add the rest of the ingredients. Cook until just tender. Drain and refrigerate.

DRESSING

Make the dressing the day before.

Ingredients
1 cup oil
¼ cup white vinegar
3 tablespoons lemon juice
1 teaspoon freshly ground pepper
1 teaspoon paprika
1 teaspoon Colman's dry mustard
2 garlic cloves
1 tablespoon dill seed

Combine all the above in a jar. Shake well and then refrigerate overnight.

ASSEMBLY

Ingredients
1 pound bacon, fried and crumbled
1 bunch green onions, sliced
2 packages (4 ounces each) crumbled Roquefort cheese
¼ cup homemade mayonnaise
2 tablespoons sour cream
¼ cup dressing (the one you made yesterday)

Add the drained green beans to a large serving bowl. Be sure you have removed the onion/ham that you cooked with the beans. Add about ¼ of the bacon and the sliced green onions. Mix the Roquefort, dressing, mayonnaise, and sour cream.

Gently fold into the bean mixture. Refrigerate several hours

before serving. Just before serving, garnish with crumbled bacon and freshly ground pepper.

You have enough dressing to at least double this recipe. Serves eight.

Greenville Green Beans

We love green beans down here! The reason they are so frequently served at parties may be that you can always get them at the grocery, which is not the case with asparagus or artichokes. Also, they are inexpensive. All these parties can get expensive, particularly when tenderloin is the meat. Older ladies tend to be tight about money. Don't ever come between them and their money, their bourbon, or their son!

Ingredients
2 pounds green beans or 2 cans (15½ ounces each) whole green
beans, rinsed and drained
Bacon slices, cut in half

If you use fresh green beans, cook them in a small amount of seasoned water until just tender. If you use the canned variety, rinse the beans, discard the canned juice, and use tap water to heat them through. Wrap a slice of bacon around 6 to 8 beans. Secure the bundle with a toothpick.

Arrange the bean bundles on a foil-covered jelly roll pan. Broil until the bacon is done. Pour hot sauce over the beans and heat for another minute or two.

SAUCE

Ingredients
3 tablespoons bacon grease
3 tablespoons cider vinegar
2 tablespoons tarragon vinegar
1 teaspoon salt
1 teaspoon paprika
1 tablespoon chopped parsley
1 teaspoon grated onion

Combine the above ingredients and bring to a boil. Boil for about 5 minutes before pouring over the beans.

Lord, do not forget to remove the toothpicks!

Seven-Layer Torte

This is something Anne Call loved to make. She liked it because "the longer it sits, the better it gets," or as we say, "gits." Also, the layers are reminiscent of old-fashioned tea cakes.

~~~~

Ingredients
3 cups sifted all-purpose flour
¾ cup sugar
2 sticks unsalted butter
1 egg

Preheat the oven to 350°.

Combine the flour and sugar. Cut the butter into this mixture until it resembles coarse cornmeal. Add the egg and blend on a low speed. Separate the dough into 7 balls. Roll each (on a lightly floured surface) into an 8-inch round approximately. Gently transfer to a baking sheet and bake at 350° until the edges are just brown (about 10 minutes). Allow to cool. If you use several baking sheets, the process moves faster.

FILLING

Ingredients
3 cups chopped pecans
3 cups sour cream

2¼ cups confectioners' sugar
1½ teaspoon vanilla

Combine the above ingredients.

Spread ½ cup (heaping) over each baked circle, stacking one on top of the other: layer, filling, layer, filling, etc. Wrap the stack well and chill overnight if possible.

Just before serving, dust the top with confectioners' sugar. I put a doily on top and sprinkle the sugar over it. Remove the doily, and you have a nice design.

Serves ten.

Cotton Boll Candy

One groom's mother was determined to show us how thoroughly she fit into the Delta way of life. She entertained at the Leland Garden Club's house. There were burlap tablecloths (à la croaker sacks) and cotton bales as decoration. Soy beans, cotton stalks, and corn were mixed with zinnias and sunflowers for floral arrangements to present a Delta landscape. Candy fashioned to look like cotton bolls were served with after-dinner coffee. It was a nice touch and impressed all the visitors who came from far north.

Our local cake baking supply shop, Patti-Cake, sells candy molds in every shape . . . even cotton bolls. To be perfectly honest, this is great-looking candy (if you're into cotton bolls), but for taste, you might prefer a more heavenly divinity.

Ingredients
1 bag (1 pound) chocolate candy molding wafers
1 bag (1 pound) white candy molding wafers

Melt the chocolate wafers first. You will use this to paint the stems.

Place a small number of wafers in a wide-mouth glass jar.

Put the jar in a saucepan that is filled about halfway up the jar with water.

Cook on simmer until the wafers have melted. As the wafers melt, stir and add a few more to the jar. Do not allow the water to boil. Use a stiff watercolor brush to apply the chocolate to the stem portion of the mold. Then proceed to the white wafers and—voila!—two-toned cotton bolls.

Using a small spoon, put enough white candy into each mold to fill. Smooth.

Tap the mold to remove any air bubbles.

Place in the freezer for 10 minutes or so.

To remove the candy, invert the mold on waxed paper, tap the bottom, and the candy will drop.

Makes about three dozen.

Julia Morgan Hall Hays' Heavenly Divinity

"I'm sure there are some ladies who like to cook," Julia Morgan Hall Hays remarked dismissively from time to time. She was not one of them. Though Julia Morgan died in 1990, we know she would like to be included in this book. And all non-cooks have a few special recipes that they do to perfection. Julia Morgan made wonderful divinity. She cooked it competitively for the St. James' bazaar, always avidly awaiting battle-front reports on how her divinity was selling, as compared to that of her sisters-in-law, both accomplished cooks. This divinity is nice with after-dinner coffee. It has been said that people who make divinity can't make anything else. Not entirely true. Julia Morgan also made caramel candy and baked apples with red-hot candies. You boil them with the red hots and then stuff them with cream cheese and nuts.

A word to the wise: Don't make divinity on a rainy day, and don't store the product in an airtight container. You can also color the divinity to match the bridesmaids' dresses, but beware of using too much color. We say stick with bridal white. But if the bride was a sireen, why not red-hot apples for the rehearsal dinner? Just kidding.

(recipe continues on next page)

Ingredients
2 cups sugar
½ cup water
½ cup white corn syrup
2 egg whites, stiffly beaten
1 teaspoon vanilla
½ cup chopped nuts

Boil sugar, water, and syrup in a heavy saucepan. When the candy thermometer reaches 250°/ hard ball stage, remove from heat. With a hand mixer on low speed, add the syrup mixture to the egg whites. It's like mayonnaise . . . keep a steady stream. Up the speed of the mixer, and beat until stiff peaks form and the mixture holds it shape. Add the vanilla, coloring (if you must), and chopped nuts. Drop by teaspoon onto waxed paper and allow to cool.

Makes twenty-four small pieces or about twenty average-sized pieces.

DELTA WEDDING HIT PARADE

Don'ts

"Love Me Tender," Elvis Presley
"Ebb Tide," Frank Sinatra or Righteous Brothers
"I Do (Cherish You)," Mark Wills
"Hail State," Mississippi State's fight song
"My Heart Will Go On," theme song from *Titanic*
Anything by Celine Dion
"When a Man Loves a Woman," Percy Sledge
"I Don't Wanna Miss a Thing," Aerosmith
"Bull Dog Rag," by Geraldine Dobyns, fine for
    MSU's Bull Dogs, but not your wedding!
"One Hand, One Heart," from *West Side Story*
"Here Comes the Bride," *Lohengrin*

Do's

Pachelbel's Canon (before the service—no, this is
    not the one with cannons booming)
"Sheep May Safely Graze," J. S. Bach (also before
    the service—and, even though it would be
    better if it were about cows, this one is still
    great for any agrarian society!)

continued

Do's

"Jesu, Joy of Man's Desiring," J. S. Bach

Trumpet Voluntary in D, Clark

"Here Comes the Bride," *Lohengrin* (only if you
absolutely must—see above)

Trumpet Tune in D, Purcell (The Purcells—aren't
they from Virginia?)

Overture to Royal Fireworks Music, Handel
(maybe better in those days when girls were
expecting fireworks that night?)

Allegro Maestoso from *Water Music Suite,* Handel
(at the departure)

"Now Thank We All Our God," Karg-Elerg or
Bach/Fox (when performed at a wedding, we're
tempted to call it "Now Thank We All Our
God—That's It's All Over!")

4

The Society Baptists: What Happens When Your Unity Candle Burns Hotter than the Bad Place?

ALTHOUGH OLD-LINE BAPTISTS and the more uptight Methodists deplore the unity candle—a relatively new feature at the Delta wedding—they have been powerless to snuff it out. Indeed, perhaps the single most compelling reason for discerning parents to join St. James' Episcopal Church before it is too late is that God's Frozen People would just as soon torch their house of worship as permit a tacky old unity candle. It should be noted that several Baptist churches have come perilously close to being transformed into the fiery furnace of Old Testament fame because they *do* allow the unity candle. Where are Shadrach, Meshach, and Abednego when you really need them . . . as firefighters?

Though one prominent Baptist wedding guru describes the unity candle as "nothing but trouble," all too many Delta brides would prefer living in sin to getting married without one. Let the snoots persist in viewing the precious candle as the ultimate sin—or, as they would no doubt put it, the ultimate faux pas— these brides demand that special Flick Your Bic moment before embarking on the marital path. The idea behind the unity candle is simple—and sentimental, which is why it has made no headway among our stodgier citizens. It is said that two grooms have a better chance of being united at dear old St. James' than a bride and groom with a unity candle.

According to unity candle protocol, the mothers of the bride and groom ascend the steps to the sanctuary and light small candles before they take their places. Shortly before they are "pronounced" (in the parlance of Baptist wedding gurus), the bride and groom light one big candle—"that big fat ugly candle," as one disgruntled bridal adviser puts it—which is the unity candle, each taking a light from the appropriate maternal flame. The ceremony can be further drawn out if the bride and groom choose to present roses to their respective mothers on the way down the aisle, whispering, "I love you," ostentatiously mouthing the words.

All this folderol is supposed to symbolize the joining of the two families. As symbolism, however, the unity candle needs some rethinking. For example, what does it symbolize when, as all too often happens, the candles flatly refuse to be lighted? Or when they flicker dangerously low and then blow out during the ceremony? Every now and then a unity candle flops over and falls on the floor. One hapless bride's gown caught on fire and the ceremony had to be halted until the fire was stamped out by frantic members of the wedding party. The lighting ceremony can be accompanied by a hymn, and no matter what hymn the bride picks, the unity candle will find a way to make it the wrong song: If it's a short hymn, the candle just won't be lit and you have the mother trying to perform her incendiary task in utter silence after the hymn is completed. "You Light Up My Life," a popular Baptist wedding tune, inevitably has people thinking: Don't light up my life, just light that blankety-blank candle so we can get on with this wedding. If a longish hymn has been chosen, the candle always seems to burst into flames on the first attempt, which can make "Sweet Hour of Prayer," an old-fashioned number, feel like several hours. Mortified mothers sometimes hold up the procession fiddling with a wily wick. Once, when a mother faced a particularly challenging wick, the Baptist preacher had to step in and rescue her. Gently moving her aside, he ignited the candle himself—with his cigarette lighter. This was perhaps not a wise idea—you could see what the congregation, previously unaware that their spiritual leader was a nicotine-addled devotee of the Satanic weed, was thinking: Next thing you know, Brother Gillis is going to take up dancing.

While some innocent brides can be forgiven for inflicting the awkwardness of a unity candle on the unsuspecting flock, one bridal consultant has yet to summon Christian charity toward a bride who, in the consultant's opinion, had no right whatsoever to the unity candle. She and the groom had already unified, as was quite obvious from her bulging condition. Don't believe an Empire waistline can conceal everything. That must be why the unity candle fell over on her head. "Served her right," said the still-bitter bridal consultant.

For guests from more scripted liturgical traditions, the second-least favorite moment of a Baptist wedding comes when the bride and groom, now husband and wife, turn around to leave the church and the preacher says, "And now presenting Mr. and Mrs. John Doe . . ." to tumultuous applause and the occasional catcall. At one such wedding, the bride and groom were "presented" as Mr. and Mrs. Girl's Last Name. Seems the father of the bride was what is known in Southern idiom as "a big Baptist," and the preacher made a little Freudian slip!

All Southern towns of any size have an elite Baptist set, recognized in the community as society Baptists, starchy stalwarts of the community who aren't any fonder of the nefarious unity candle than traditionalists in other denominations. The social Baptists are confronted by the same blond wood pews—for some reason, Baptists love blond wood—and odd geography (there is no central aisle, and the bride must come in from the left) that beset humbler members of their faith. But they surmount these obstacles with aplomb. They try to pretend the TV camera (for broadcasting the minister's sermon) isn't there and substitute "Jesu, Joy of Man's Desiring" for a schmaltzy solo rendition of the Lord's Prayer, otherwise the hallmark of the Baptist wedding. Incongruously enough, Baptists also like Ave Maria, hailed in one Baptist newspaper write-up as Ava Maria, which sounds suspiciously like one of those double-barreled Southern girl's names.

The society Baptists choose fresh flowers over the eternal flowers popular at other Baptist weddings. (Fresh flowers are particularly useful in disguising the immersion pool.) Brother

Gillis is quietly (but firmly) informed that he'd better keep his extemporaneous remarks to a minimum.

One of the greatest Delta weddings of yesteryear was, in fact, that of a social Baptist, whose family decked the Baptist church of Leland in so many flowers that nobody saw a speck of blond wood. There were bouquets on the rails leading into the church and a canopy of roses overhead. The bride wore a gown from Worth in Paris, which looked all the more beautiful in the shimmering glow from the cathedral candles. "It was so beautiful, it didn't look like a Baptist wedding," said a disloyal Leland Baptist. There was one small imperfection in planning: The preacher was stationed directly below one of the larger candles, and it dripped globs of hot wax onto his bald head throughout the service. At least it wasn't a unity candle!

Although there are more Baptist churches than liquor stores in Greenville, non-Baptists find Baptists exotic. We are fascinated with two aspects of Baptist life: their drinking habits— we'll get to that in a second—and their famous immersion pool. When Polly Billings, the daughter of one of Greenville's most upright families among the social Baptists, showed her little friends the immersion pool one Saturday, they couldn't have been more titillated if they'd been to an adult book store. An erstwhile Methodist decided to take the dip last year because of his lady friend. "She didn't want to commit adultery with somebody who wasn't a Baptist," he explained. First Baptist, by the way, is the church that attracts the doctors and lawyers and more erudite of the local Baptists. But some of the blue-haired Sunday school teachers, sweet though they are, could be more learned. Dr. Billings realized that he had a burgeoning Episcopalian or Presbyterian on his hands when Margaret Billings came home from Sunday school and announced that old Mrs. Hicks had taught the lesson about Simon the Leapfrog that morning in Sunday school. Maybe the old lady got Jeremiah the prophet confused with Jeremiah the bullfrog and threw in Simon Peter for good measure?

When people in the Delta receive an invitation to a Baptist wedding, social or otherwise, their first question is: Will they serve liquor? Episcopalians in particular are convinced that the main reason Baptists don't drink is to annoy Episcopalians. A deacon of the First Baptist Church was chosen as king of the Queen of Hearts Ball, one of Greenville's highest social honors, a few years ago. When King Deacon insisted that the demon rum (and all other demons of an alcoholic nature) be banished from the king's table, Mr. Buddy Gilliam angrily insisted that the deacon had been a Baptist all his life just to avoid paying a liquor bill for that one night!

Alternative dogma on Baptists: They are *all* secret drinkers. "Or they think it's a secret," huffs a prominent matron of another faith. One of our town's favorite Baptist jokes: Where do Baptists not recognize each other? At the liquor store. Of course, this is a canard and not in the least bit fair—many Delta Baptists, being as much Delta as Baptist, do drink, and openly. The rule: If a Baptist reception is at the Fellowship Hall, it will be dry, as dry as Pharaoh's desert, but if it is elsewhere, alcoholic beverages will likely flow like the river Jordan.

We must point out that there are exceptions to this rule. A

nice Baptist family was hosting a reception in the Fellowship Hall a few years ago, and one of the guests, partaking from his flask in the parking lot (a parking lot is sort of a bar for Baptists), became inspired with an idea of how to enliven the affair. He staggered into the Fellowship Hall and tossed his flask into the mint-green punch, in that instant ensuring it became the first (and last) spiked punch served in the Fellowship Hall. Even if it did seem to enhance fellowship.

At a country club reception in another Delta town, the Baptist hosts had removed *all* the liquor bottles from the shelves in the bar. Even looking at the stuff might tempt you to sin. The food was lovely and elaborate, washed down with iced tea and water (without even a lemon wedge!). The band was playing, but no one was dancing. We thought it was because everybody was stone-cold sober. But then it dawned on us: Dancing is a sin. That must be why the Baptist girls are always the best dancers—a soupçon of sin makes any activity more fun. "Baptist girls are sugar-coated hellcats with two hollow legs," says an appreciative member of male society. Baptists, of course, are very serious about their faith, and that is why we all worried that a prominent Baptist dentist, a particularly observant citizen, was trying to send us subliminal Baptist messages while he worked on our teeth. Of course, there was nothing subliminal about it—it was the scenes from the Bible painted on the ceiling above the dental chair combined with the Demerol that turned our thoughts to higher matters.

A Baptist wedding, with fresh flowers and traditional hymns, perhaps outside with a gentle breeze rippling through the trees, can be a quintessential Delta experience—but, because the ceremony is not as by-the-book as it is in other denominations, Baptists must think things through with particular attention to detail. One of our sweetest brides wanted to honor her late grandmother, a popular Greenville matriarch. She decided to have Granny's favorite hymn sung at her wedding. The bride and groom stood, hand in hand, gazing meaningfully into each other's eyes, as the soloist belted out "I'd Rather Have Jesus."

An oddity of the Delta bride is that she loves to sing—sometimes at her own wedding. One Greenville socialite insisted upon an elaborate wedding, held at an ancestral residence with an imposing staircase—at the top of which she sang "O Perfect Love, All Human Thought Transcending," before stepping back to take her father's arm and all the stairs descending. A memorable moment, to say the least.

We know another bride who dreamed of a wedding in a beautiful country chapel. She had forgotten that a big train runs past the little church every day—at the precise moment the couple was to recite their vows. Nobody heard a word they said. The engine not only drowned out their promises before God, its rumbling also caused a large floral cross to fall from on high in the sanctuary.

A wedding is never the time to be creative. We, for example, might have advised Phyllis Philpot, a Methodist bride from Rolling Fork, Mississippi, that having the ring bearer carry the ring up the aisle on deer's antlers does not constitute impeccable taste. But she didn't ask us. We might also have counseled restraint for the couple who, as did another pair mentioned earlier, insisted upon being married on horseback. "The ceremony was somewhat different," the newspaper reported, "in that the minister, as a favor of the bride and groom, offered to all those attending who wished to an opportunity to renew their vows." *That's* what he thought was different?

Baptists, as you may be beginning to see, all too often go in for so many special effects that you almost expect the credits to roll as the couple walks down the aisle—wedding by Cecil B. DeBaptist. A Baptist wedding in Clarksdale, for example, featured soloists stationed in the sanctuary and others leaning over the balcony—voices from heaven?—who sang back and forth. Needless to say, all wore microphones, which somehow did not add to the overall aesthetic effect. An elevated platform had been built at the center pew (prime seating) to hold the video equipment—as if anybody could ever forget this wedding. A word about videographers: They are wedding villains, always popping out from the palms in the sanctuary to capture—or ruin—some magic moment. The video of the wedding has become more important than the wedding—as clearly illustrated by the pregnant bride who waited until after her child was born to wed the father. She wanted to look slim in her wedding video. In the old days, we had Flash Carson, the town's society lens man, ambling up and down the aisle, setting off his eponymous bulbs at the most inopportune times. That was bad enough. Immortalizing a wedding today seems to demand a fleet of equipment-wielding techies. It's enough to make us pine for the simpler days of Flash.

There is also the perfectly nice wedding that goes bad in the telling of it. A recent write-up of a "storybook wedding" praised a wedding coordinator who "orchestrated the enormous task of placement of so many tents and executive bathrooms to adhere to the wishes of the bride's mother not to cut down any trees."

We may feel we've been to an elegant wedding when the rental agency from Jackson has to bring potties—but it's not necessary to read about potty *placement* in the newspaper. Nor are we interested in post-reception details about the newlyweds. When Maribelle Gordon married that lout Harwood Swinton, we did not need to know that "around midnight, the bride and groom slipped away to the Marriott." "I'm just glad Mama didn't live to read that," said Miss Ardelia Stovall, Maribelle's aunt.

One other tip: If you're going to wear something tacky to your own wedding, there is no need to inform the whole world and posterity. We are hoping that one man we know will burn his wedding write-up so that his children will never know that he wore—and we quote—"a polyester double knit suit designed by Pierre Cardin with appropriate accessories and black leather Italian boots" to the "after reception." Please, if you know what an "after reception" is, don't tell us.

A MORNING COFFEE PARTY MENU

A MORNING coffee party is one of the nicest ways to entertain a bride. Baptists particularly dote on this alcohol-free mode of celebrating a betrothal. Could that be because they feel better than the rest of us in the morning hours? For a recent bridal party, the hostess served coffee in the dining room and lemonade in the garden. A striped tent had been erected because the older ladies, not a generation of sun-worshippers, otherwise would have baked. A delicious coffee and marshmallow concoction (see page 135 for recipe) was served in antique demitasse cups with silver demitasse spoons. The mixture was chosen in honor of the well-known Baptist fondness for cooking with itty-bitty marshmallows, their signature ingredient in festive dishes. We think the white, fluffy 'mallows remind them of being pure as the driven snow. The garnish was flavored whipped cream (no alcohol!) and chocolate shavings. You can make this two days in advance, if you have enough refrigerator space.

Needless to say, there were our ubiquitous fried walnuts (page 209) and cheese straws (without which the proper Delta hostess cannot entertain). Everything else was

continued

passed by the hostesses and their friends, with the exception of the coffee. The coffee was poured from a silver coffeepot that was part of an old silver service (a silver service was once the standard, big-ticket wedding present for all brides, but what with the skyrocketing silver prices, that is but a memory!). It was placed at one end of the dining table. At the other end of the table, on a matching tray, was the Coeur à la Crème. A morning coffee was probably the best way to entertain this fairly large gathering.

Coffee Pot de Crème for Demitasse Cups

When you put itsy-bitsy marshmallows in this elegant French dessert, should you call it pot de cream? Whatever you call it, it's delicious. We serve it with an alcohol-laced whipped cream and a small cookie. Do not be too proud to serve this. We've had many a food snob tell us it's delicious.

~~~~

Ingredients
¾ cup leftover strong coffee
½ pound mini marshmallows
1 cup heavy cream, whipped
Pinch of salt

TOPPING

1 cup heavy cream, whipped
Confectioners' sugar to taste
1 teaspoon vanilla
Bourbon or rum to taste

Heat coffee in a double boiler. Add marshmallows and stir until dissolved.

Using a hand mixer, beat the mixture until foamy and then stir in salt.

Fold in the whipped cream. Be sure the marshmallows are so

completely absorbed that you don't have to reveal you used this plebeian ingredient. Fill the pots de crème to within an inch or so of the top. Put the tops on and refrigerate overnight. Before serving, whip the cream and add confectioners' sugar to taste. Fold in the vanilla and add enough bourbon or rum to taste. You must really flavor the cream.

Remove tops, nap with flavored whipped cream, and replace the tops. The original recipe calls for a chocolate curl or shavings. I prefer to serve with a tiny cookie or a fried walnut or two.

A word about serving: Southern ladies love demitasse cups, pots de crème, and tiny cream soup cups. But men rarely appreciate them. Either they don't hold enough, or men can't get their fingers through the rings. DO NOT use tiny cups for a groom candidate. But for a morning coffee for ladies, you can't do better.

Makes twelve.

Red Pepper Lemonade

The lemonade, garnished only with mint grown in the yard, was served in cool crystal flutes, placed on a round table in the tent. It was just plain lemonade, but very tasty. However, if you want something jazzier, this is an excellent alternative to the traditional lemonade.

~~~~

Ingredients
2 cups fresh lemon juice
1½ cups pure maple syrup
8 cups water
½ teaspoon ground red pepper

Mix the lemon juice and maple syrup. Add the water, mixing well. Stir in the red pepper, add ice, and serve. The pepper perks matters up a bit!

Makes fourteen eight-ounce servings.

Cream Puffs (Southern for Pate à Choux)

Do not be intimidated. These are so easy and serve many purposes beyond the custard filling. For this morning coffee, we used egg salad. You can make these in advance and freeze, but they must be reheated before being filled.

~~~~

Ingredients
1 cup flour
½ teaspoon salt
¾ tsp sugar (or less)
1 cup water
1 stick unsalted butter, cut in pieces
4 large eggs

Combine flour, salt, and sugar. In a medium saucepan boil the water, and as it boils add the pieces of butter, one at a time. After the last piece has melted, add the flour mixture. Stir until smooth and the mixture forms a ball. Remove the pan from the heat and allow to sit for 2 or 3 minutes.

Add 1 egg at a time, beating well after each addition.

After the eggs have been incorporated, stir no more, as you will over-mix and affect the rising. Allow to rest 5 minutes or so.

Preheat the oven to 350°.

You can bake these directly on a sheet. However, using parchment paper to cover the bottom of the baking sheet prevents the bottoms from getting too dark. Times change, so today there are no more trips to Memphis or Jackson—simply head to your local Wally World for parchment paper.

Use a small teaspoon to drop the pastry onto the parchment-covered baking sheet. Keep the puffs small (you know small is always better) and space them about 2 inches apart.

To ensure a nice glaze, mix a large egg with 1 teaspoon water. Brush the top of each puff . . . gently. Southern cooks prefer using their hands instead of a pastry brush. Simply dip your finger in the egg wash. No one has complained or died—yet! You have more control when not using a pastry brush.

Bake at 350° for approximately 17 minutes. You can tell if they are not ready, if when you remove one from the oven, it collapses. If you make larger puffs, increase the cooking time to 20 minutes. When cool, split in half and fill with the desired filling. I prefer waiting to fill until just before serving, as some fillings will make the bottoms soggy.

Makes approximately 3 dozen small.

EGG SALAD FILLING

Ingredients
6 eggs, hard-boiled, peeled, and chopped
1 stalk celery, chopped
1 green onion, minced (optional)
½ cup homemade mayonnaise, or to taste

2 tablespoons cream cheese
1 slice crumbled bacon
Pinch of tarragon
Salt and white pepper to taste

Combine the above ingredients and allow mixture to sit covered in the icebox for several hours before serving . . . we think the flavors like to get friendly with each other.

Good egg salad really doesn't require much; perhaps just mayo and salt. However, there are many versions. Some people like to add fig chutney, shredded cheddar cheese, sliced or chopped olives (black or pimiento stuffed), or curry powder.

GOAT CHEESE AND SUN-DRIED TOMATO FILLING

Ingredients
11 ounces goat cheese (Chèvre)
½ cup sun-dried tomatoes, well drained
1 heaping tablespoon basil pesto
Pinch of fresh rosemary (optional)

Blend all ingredients. Refrigerate until ready to use.

Chicken Salad
for Cream Puffs or Tartlets

We didn't serve this, but it is another ideal filling, if the party is later in the day.

~~~~

Ingredients
6 chicken breasts (this equals about eight cups finely chopped)
1 medium onion, quartered
1 carrot
1 stalk celery with top
1 chicken bouillon cube
Peppercorns

Cover the breasts with water. Add onion, carrot, celery (with top), bouillon cube, and several peppercorns. Bring the water to a boil and then reduce to simmer. Cook until the chicken is completely done.

Remove chicken and with your kitchen shears (I love my Joyce Chen shears) cut the meat into very small pieces. Remember this chicken salad is for small tart shells or cream puffs.

If you choose to use this for a luncheon dish, leave the chicken in nice chunks. Add a white grape or two.

DRESSING

Ingredients
1 cup homemade mayonnaise
4 ounces cream cheese
⅓ cup sour cream
2 tablespoons fresh lemon juice
1 teaspoon dried tarragon

Blend the above ingredients.
Refrigerate.

Makes one and a quarter cups.

CHICKEN SALAD FILLING

Ingredients
½ cup homemade mayonnaise
3 green onions, chopped
1 cup finely chopped celery
1 cup toasted slivered almonds
¼ teaspoon cayenne pepper
1 teaspoon white pepper
½ teaspoon salt
1 tablespoon fresh lemon juice

Add the above ingredients to the chopped chicken, followed by the addition of the dressing (which you made the day before). Mix well.

Cover and refrigerate before serving.

Makes five cups of chicken salad.

Coeur à la Crème

It doesn't take much for a Southerner to get into a theme, and a wedding is the perfect place to go crazy (for one reason or other). We served this because it is heart-shaped and delicious. It's quite possible that none of the younger guests knew what it was. That's the reason it's always good to have a blend of ages.

Use a white porcelain heart-shaped mold with holes in the bottom, the traditional Coeur à la crème mold. This one holds about three quarts. Line the mold with a double thickness of cheesecloth, leaving enough to fold over and cover the top.

~~~~

Ingredients
1 box (8 ounces) Philadelphia cream cheese
1¾ cups cottage cheese
½ cup sour cream
2 tablespoons confectioners' sugar
Pinch salt
½ cup heavy cream, whipped

In the food processor blend cream cheese, cottage cheese, sour cream, sugar, and salt.

Process until smooth, fold in the whipped cream. Transfer to the mold and pack to remove any air bubbles. Fold cheesecloth over the top. Set the mold on a plate to catch any drippings and refrigerate overnight. Unmold this onto a large serving tray, removing the cheesecloth gently.

Serves 25 as finger food.

W E used a silver tray and served three kinds of strawberries . . . dipped in white chocolate, dark chocolate, and plain. We dragged out Ann Call's sugar caster and sifted the powdered sugar for it. We used heart-shaped toast points, black bread, and white bread that had been lightly toasted. The contrasts of white and black and red were lovely.

WHITE CHOCOLATE AND DARK CHOCOLATE—COVERED STRAWBERRIES

M ELT semisweet chocolate in a small saucepan over medium heat. Do not let the chocolate get too hot. Stir gently until the chocolate is melted. Remove from heat and dip the tip of each strawberry, about one-third to one-half the way up. Try to leave the leaves and stem on the berry.

Open-Faced Cucumber Sandwiches

English cucumbers are long, skinny, and seedless. The ones we grow in the Delta are fatter and with seeds. Either variety should be peeled, thinly sliced, and soaked overnight in a mixture of ice water and white vinegar. I use half vinegar and half water to which a bit of salt has been added.

~~~~

Ingredients
Cucumbers
Wheat bread
Unsalted butter, softened
Homemade mayonnaise
Paprika

Using a small heart cookie cutter, cut the cucumber and the bread the same size.

Butter the bread, spread with mayonnaise.

Pat the cucumbers dry and put on top of the mayo. If you are not serving the sandwiches for a while, cover them with a damp tea towel. Just before serving, sprinkle with paprika.

Osceola Coffee Punch

We are cheating a bit by including this recipe—we actually served regular coffee at our party. But this would be an excellent addition to a morning coffee. The recipe comes from one of the great cookbooks of our region, the beloved *Gourmet of the Delta*. The late Mrs. Lawrence Lipscomb Paxton, once a prominent hostess, contributed this recipe. Osceola was the name of her house. This is lovely served in a silver punch bowl.

Ingredients
1 cup milk
1 small (two-ounce) jar instant coffee
2 quarts chocolate ice cream
2 quarts vanilla ice cream
1 pint home-style vanilla ice cream
1 pint heavy cream, whipped
Chocolate sauce
Nutmeg

Bring the milk to a boil and add the coffee. Stir until dissolved. Cool completely.

Blend milk/coffee mixture and the 4 quarts of ice creams. Pour into punch bowl and chill in the freezer. Just before serving, float the softened home-style vanilla ice cream in the punch with the whipped cream on top. Drizzle with chocolate sauce and sprinkle lightly with a few gratings of fresh nutmeg.

Makes about thirty servings.

SOMETHING BOUGHT

PETIT fours with ivory fondant icing completed the menu. Petit fours can be larger, but these were tiny, maybe an inch square. They were monogrammed with the first letter of the bride's surname in soft pink and her surname-to-be (if she takes his name) in a mossy green that is known in Greenville as Kyle green, after the favorite color of the late Kyle Pickens, a popular Delta interior designer. Did we make these? Sometimes the better part of being a good hostess is knowing that some things are better bought than homemade. Petit fours come in this category.

Evelyn Hall's Swits

Evelyn Hall was Anne Gayden Call's best friend (and Charlotte's aunt). Mother didn't make these, because Evelyn always brought them to her. I can remember looking for the tin from Bourbon, Mississippi—where Evelyn lived. If the Halls had a really good pecan crop, Evelyn would stuff each date with a pecan. Swits is the old-fashioned name for these tiny pickups.

~~~~

Ingredients
1 stick unsalted butter, softened
1/2 pound extra-sharp Cheddar cheese, grated
1 1/2 cups flour
1/2 teaspoon salt
1 teaspoon red pepper
1 eight-ounce bag dates
1/2 cup confectioners' sugar (optional)

Preheat the oven to 400°.

Blend butter and cheese. Add flour, salt, red pepper. Mix until incorporated, but not too much or your dough will be tough. Pinch off small amounts and cover each date, sealing the edges well. Bake at 400° until lighly browned, about 12 minutes or so. If desired, when cool, sprinkle lightly with confectioners' sugar.

Church Punch

But which church? Southerners refer to the punch made with green sherbet, so beloved of our childhood, as Presbyterian Punch. (A recipe for Presbyterian Punch is on page 221.) This isn't the traditional Presbyterian Punch—it has Kool-Aid, which makes us think more of Jim Jones than John Calvin. We know maraschino cherries and Kool-Aid are tacky. But, if you give it a chance, it's quite tasty—and maybe you can spike it when nobody's looking. Then it really tastes good.

~~~~

Ingredients
1 quart very warm water
3 cups sugar
4 packages (23 ounces each) Kool-Aid
2 cans (46 ounces each) pineapple juice (don't forget to save the cans)
1 can (14 ounces) frozen lemon juice, defrosted
4 cups cranberry or cranberry-apple juice
6 quarts ginger ale, chilled

Maraschino cherries, well drained (optional), but cranberries would be a bit more dignified.

Dissolve the sugar in warm water.

Add the Kool-Aid and stir. Then add the pineapple juice,

lemon juice, and cranberry juice. After well mixed, pour back into the pineapple juice cans (you will need extra containers). Put in the freezer. As the mixture freezes, you can add well-drained maraschino cherries (or cranberries).

At least 2 hours before serving, remove from the freezer and let thaw. You can immerse these cans in hot water to speed the process, but be sure to thaw just enough to loosen the mold from the can. Place two of the frozen molds in the punch bowl and pour chilled ginger ale over them. Gently break up the molds to create a very slushy punch.

Makes about three gallons.

HOW TO GIVE YOUR PUNCH MORE PUNCH ̄WITHOUT ADDING ALCOHOL:

Any punch can be enhanced by the addition of an ice or punch mold. Simply freeze plain water or some of the punch (with perhaps a few tiny flowers or bits of fruit) in a round mold. Before the reception begins, unmold and float in the punch bowl.

An ice or punch mold will ensure that the punch does not get lukewarm, a real no-no.

WEDDING FLOWERS

Don'ts

All Tropicals—Do you really want a phallic symbol
bouquet at your wedding?

Glads—so tacky they'd make us sads

Blood Red Roses—There are so many beautiful
colors we don't know why anybody buys El
Tacko roses.

Forever Flowers . . . you know, the nonbiodegradable
kind that will still be "alive" for your funeral

Corsages—We wish we could dissuade the DAR
ladies from wearing orchids from hell (also
known as cymbidiums) on their large Daughter
bosoms. If Grandmother demands a corsage, it
should be small and worn attached to a purse or
hankie.

Leather leaf, a fernlike filler that looks like plastic
and just might be

A single anything—looks like you're being cheap!
The single rose lost its meaning around the time
of Robbie Burns.

continued

Baby's breath (can become a "do" if used very
sparingly or as circlet of flowers for younger
members of the wedding party)

Daisies—unless you're getting married in a field (If
you use daisies, use only a few and be sure they
are not dyed.)

Plastic bouquet holders . . . those things the florist
calls a shortcut. They just cram the flowers in
and hope for the best.

Anything with glitter!

Do's: Bring Back the Tussie-Mussie

A scent wedding—Certain fresh flowers can be
chosen to give a lovely scent—just be sure they
are not overwhelming.

Herbs—such as a sprig of rosemary for
remembrance

Lilies (especially lily of the valley), roses (gentle
colors), sweet peas, hydrangeas (the beautiful
green ones)

A garland of boxwoods, which we call box. The
young attendants carry the garlands and attach
them to family pews and choir stalls.

continued

Wrapped stems, hand-tied, with a beautiful ribbon
or a lovely handkerchief, one from your
grandmother, if possible. A lovely baby pin or
some other trinket of meaning incorporated
into the bouquet, as long as it's not schmaltzy.

Arm bouquets

Beautiful ribbon

Garden flowers and greenery

Love knots down the ribbons of the bouquet

And, of course, a tussie-mussie—A tussie-mussie
is a small, cornucopia-shaped flower holder.
Victorian brides carried them, and we're
encouraging a tussie-mussie revival.

5

~~~~

The Shotgun Wedding:
Do You Know Who Mah Daddy Is?

ALTHOUGH THE TERM "shotgun wedding" is used as a metaphor for a forced or unlikely union in many parts of the country, in the Delta, a famous shotgun wedding involved an actual shotgun. A non-PETA-approved, ten-gauge shotgun was in the hands of Otis Bilbo Landreth (of the correctionally challenged Landreths) the night he and his twin sons, Wayne and DeWayne, banged loud enough to wake the dead on the ancestral front door of Young Buck From a Fine Old Delta Family. Young Buck had made the mistake of taking Mae Landreth to not watch a movie at the old Joy Drive-in Theater (pronounced: thee-a-ter) on Highway 82. The Joy was aptly named—being possibly the most amorous patch of land in the entire Ark-La-Miss, it had brought unbridled joy to many. Couples often became so engrossed in not watching the movie that they drove off with the sound phones still attached to the car window. Some of the more fabled Delta gad-about gals proudly displayed collections of trophy sound phones in their faux–French provincial bedrooms. As a rule, Mae Landreth tried to be a Christian. She had never taken home a sound box. But she did get carried away and succumb to the charms of Young Buck the night they went to not watch *Old Yeller*. Buck dearly loved *Old Yeller*, a Disney movie for children, because it reminded him of his own dog, Gus. But he already had seen it many times. Mae did not acquire a sound phone that night, but a memento was definitely on the way.

Otis usually went to bed with the chickens—as we say down here—or at least he did before he got tight as a tick and shot the birds dead. That it was well after midnight when he paid his call to Young Buck's only showed Otis's total dedication to the task at hand: making his daughter an honest woman. Or, as Big Otis put it, "a honest woman." The minute Young Buck opened the door, he knew he was in big trouble. He was right. The Landreths dragged Buck to their pickup truck, tied him up, and took off down a long, winding road. Buck knew this might well be his last night on earth. But he had to make one desperate attempt to escape. "I have to go to the bathroom," he whimpered. The Landreth boys were not the brightest bulbs in the chandelier; they unsuspectingly pulled into the very next service station and untied Buck. As soon as Buck grasped the key safely in his trembling hand, he asked the attendant, "Would you call the police if I broke this plate-glass window?" The attendant was so rattled that he nearly dialed Sheriff Lester before Buck picked up a chair and hurled it through the window. Before the twins had figured out what caused the commotion, Young Buck had locked himself in the men's bathroom, where he remained until the sheriff knocked on the door. Of course, Buck was stunned beyond belief that the sheriff had the nerve to actually arrest *him*. "Do you know who mah daddy is?" he asked incredulously. Still, central lockup beat spending more time with the Landreths. Even so, Buck was hardly off the hook—when Buck Senior learned the cause of the midnight disturbance, he was adamant: Any son of his was damned well going to act like a gentleman and Do the Right Thing.

A quiet wedding was hastily arranged. Such weddings were traditionally celebrated in one of three places: the justice of the peace's, at home, or in the minister's house. There was no question of a big church wedding. There was no reception, or at most there might be a small and forlorn gathering. People spoke of the proceedings in hushed tones. And was Young Buck's life ruined by his impromptu nuptials? Not a bit. Buck and May— she changed the spelling, after a few gentle hints from her mother-in-law—have been happily married for many years. Sometimes Doing the Right Thing turns out just fine.

A shotgun wedding need not be a disaster. As old Mrs. Wilton Estill, a pillar of Greenville society, also knows. Like Buck and May, Mrs. Wilton Estill and Wilton, a young buck in his own right back in those days, had a very quiet wedding. Some couples like to wait awhile and settle in before they have their first child, but the Estills rushed into parenthood, adopting Wilton Jr. before their first wedding anniversary. Whenever tactless (or forgetful) people commented that the boy was the spitting image of his daddy, Mrs. Estill smiled enigmatically. She knew that a reverse of the usual difficult situation awaited her: How do you tell a child he's *not* adopted?

We do not mean to give the impression that all shotgun weddings are successful. That would be irresponsible on our part. Some are nightmares. For example, there was a couple in Arkansas that Had to Get Married. No sooner had they moved into their new trailer than the wife began cheating on her husband. He quickly found out, possibly because she made no attempt to hide it, and retaliated by wiring the trailer with explosives. He then crouched behind a tree and waited patiently—which is easy to do if you're unemployed—for the unwary Galahad to come a-calling. When he was sure his rival was far enough into the mobile home that escape was unlikely, he pushed the lever and blew the whole shebang to Kingdom Come. This clearly is an example of a shotgun wedding that did not work out well.

It's amazing that there aren't more tragic stories like this in the Delta, given the prevalence of secluded rendezvous spots. Old Farmer Pickens used to say that his "place" produced more babies than bales of cotton per acre. The land under the bridge over the Mississippi River was a close second to the Pickens farm for attracting frisky young couples. Olivia Morgan Gilliam's older daughter, however, insists that, despite the availability of venues, shotgun weddings were rare in her day (the 1950s). According to Little Olivia, two factors served to save many Delta girls from Making a Mistake: First, there was an overwhelming fear of causing a scandal that would absolutely kill your po' mo-thuh and daddy (just as soon as they got through killing you in a shotgun non-wedding). Secondly, and

perhaps more effectively, there were the Delta's vicious mosquitoes. It is very difficult to reach a pitch of passion when you are
being set upon by these sadist guardians of female virtue. The
Joy Drive-in was perspicacious enough to pass out "mosquito
coils" (tiny devices that were lighted and placed on the dash-
board), but Farmer Pickens and the levee board weren't so
thoughtful. As a result, many Delta girls who might otherwise
have shown themselves to be of easy virtue had big (and sometimes deserved) church weddings.

A Delta girl might enjoy a little sport, but she always tries to
maintain the family honor. When Little Olivia went home with a
bad beard burn one afternoon, she didn't dare use the front door,
which Papa guarded like a hawk. Instead she insisted on being
driven down the alley and climbing over the fence. She was
shocked to find big Olivia Morgan in the kitchen, not her natural
habitat. "What is wrong with your face?" she asked with alarm.
Little Olivia was so guilt-stricken that she felt she could not add
the mortal sin of lying to the sin of necking. "I was making out
under the bridge," she shamefacedly admitted. Big Olivia Morgan looked hurt. She drew herself up. "You are lying to your mo-
thuh," she said, "and that is not nice. What would people say if
they knew you lied to your mo-thuh?" An ability to deny the obvious (or a tendency to be so vague and out-of-it that vulgar reality rarely rears its ugly old head) has assured a placid passage
through life for many older belles. Even so, the vaguest of mothers were not too off in la-la land to tell their daughters that
"nothing good happens after midnight."

While we have had our share of quiet weddings featuring a

groom whom Mo-thuh might not have specifically chosen for a lifetime of dining on Aunt Belle's Wedgwood, there is also the exact opposite of the shotgun wedding. We refer, of course, to the unhappy circumstances when some unfortunate is jilted. For some reason, this seems to happen most often in Bolivar County, indicating that people there may be even crazier than in our beloved Washington County. Please understand, we don't mean that in a pejorative way. It is a compliment. Delta people take pride in having eccentric relatives. We are competitively crazy in the Delta. Lissa Clark has always maintained that, if you don't have a weird old relative locked in the attic like Mrs. Rochester in *Jane Eyre*, you aren't really from a nice family. Sadly, Lissa's efforts to lure her own aunt Betty into the attic failed and the old dear continued her habit of cooking naked in the mirrored kitchen. But they are a lovely Delta family, as you can obviously tell.

There are many lovely Delta families in Bolivar County, which is next to our county, and which has developed the most eccentric matrimonial practice in the Delta, a twist on mere jilting: returning to a previous sweetheart at the very last minute possible—or sometimes *after* the last minute possible. When Sistuh Sturdivant became engaged to a nice young man from Memphis, her mother could not have been more pleased. Mrs. Sturdivant, a leading light in both the Dames and the Daughters (are not some bosoms God-created to wear the paraphernalia of the Daughters?), set about planning the Delta wedding to end all last Delta weddings. She ordered invitations from the finest stationer in Memphis. The engraving was so deep, you practically needed to be rushed to the emergency room for stitches if you gave an invitation the finger test. The write-up received prominent display in the Memphis paper. Everything was perfect. But then Sistuh got to thinking. The more she thought, the more she knew she was still in love with her true love from high school. She was about to make a Big Mistake. She was not alone in her thoughts: Mr. High School Honey was also pining for her.

It was late in the day, but Mrs. Sturdivant quickly employed the kind of resourcefulness that has made the Delta female such an object of awe. She kept the church date and the caterer. She did not cancel the order for libations. She did, of course, order new invitation cards from the Memphis stationer. But not new envelopes. She simply (or not so simply) steamed open the original envelopes and switched invitations. It was suggested that this might seem strange, as everybody already knew about Sistuh's impending nuptials from the Memphis paper. "Oh, good heavens," Mrs. Sturdivant pooh-poohed. "Nobody remembers what they read in the paper. Who's going to notice that we have a new groom?"

One couple in Jilting County, which is what we like to call Bolivar County, was slower to realize where true love lay. It seems that after a lavish wedding they boarded the train for New York. It was quite a surprise when they returned after one night and got their marriage annulled. Both quickly married their high school sweethearts and lived happily ever after. A double jilting is pushing the envelope even for Bolivar County.

Sometimes, of course, the shotgun doesn't go off. A couple on Lake Washington, from whence our part of the world was originally settled by families from Kentucky (also known for well-bred, if not in-bred, eccentricity) were pillars of the Episcopal church. They had also been pillars of the sixties. The era, alas, had left its mark. One day in a haze, the mother took it into her head that the daughter, a local beauty, was going to marry into the richest family on Lake Washington. She started baking up a storm, and made the wedding cake. Unfortunately, Mother had neglected to inform the richest man on the lake that he was going to be her son-in-law. Fortunately, the cake froze well.

The shotgun wedding has fallen on hard times. Lax morals killed it deader than a do'nail (that's doornail to Yankees). A young girl who became PG (as our grandmothers, unable to utter the word *pregnant* in public, called it) recently, did not slink into the minister's study for a quickie—a quickie wedding, we mean. "We want to do this wedding just as big as if Marilyn wasn't with child," the mother said. She took her daughter to Memphis to try on pregnant brides' dresses. (They really exist.) It was a big wedding, and everybody had a nice time, unimpeded by the knowledge that a christening party was already in the offing. Only grandmothers are still endowed with a sense of shame. When one Greenville lady's grandson, who lived on the other side of the river—that would be anyplace west of the Mississippi—took the mother of his children to the altar a scant three weeks before the blessed arrival, the grandmother told everybody in town that young Francis and his bride had been secretly married for a year. "But Mama," the old lady's daughter demanded, "why on earth would anybody get secretly married in this day and age?" The grandmother smiled enigmatically. "Who knows?" she purred. "Aren't these young people crazy?"

Cocktail Smokies
(gourmet version)

The essence of good manners is putting others at ease. Being haughty or snobbish is bad manners. You must always pretend that whatever is served is just about the best thing you ever put in your mouth. Fortunately, little cocktail smokies, which may be just about the tackiest thing you've ever put in your mouth, are delicious. We like to imagine Mrs. Otis Bilbo Landreth serving them the first time she entertained the Bucks. We call this the gourmet version because it calls for red currant jelly instead of the usual grape. (Believe it or not, this recipe is in many of the nicest Southern cookbooks. And they all say "serve from a chafing dish." How else would you want your wieners?)

////

Ingredients
2 packages "Little Smokies"
One 10-ounce jar red currant jelly
1 small jar mustard

Combine all ingredients and heat thoroughly. Serve in a chafing dish to keep hot. Long bamboo skewers are necessary to retrieve the smokies. The bad news is that these things are always served with toothpicks! Unfortunately, that's not the only thing

Mr. Landreth uses toothpicks for. Proper etiquette: Pretend it isn't happening.

Makes thirty.

Meatballs à la Mobile Home

This would be perfect for the small, awkward reception after a shotgun wedding. Easy to prepare (even in a mobile home) and surprisingly tasty.

Shape ground beef into small meatballs. In an oven-proof dish, sauté the meatballs until brown. Drain off the fat and cover with the following sauce. Sauté until brown. Drain meatballs and set aside.

SAUCE

Ingredients
One 12-ounce bottle Heinz chili sauce
One 1-pound box brown sugar
1 small bottle vinegar
1 small bottle water

A small bottle of vinegar? Fill the emptied Heinz chili sauce bottle with vinegar, and you have a small bottle of vinegar. Do the same for the water.

Combine all ingredients. Pour the sauce over the meatballs. Cover and cook at 300° for 2½ hours in a very slow oven. Remove cover and cook for an additional 30 minutes (or until thick).

Makes twenty.

WHITE TRASH

THIS recipe comes from Mary Dayle McCormick, who with her husband, Hugh, runs Greenville's beloved McCormick Book Inn. Mary Dayle says to make twice as much as you think you'll need. You will eat half yourself, before you manage to get your delicious White Trash stored in sealed containers and ready to be delivered to the party. "If you want to get cute, you can add those pastel sugar bead thingies to match your theme colors," Mary Dayle said. "Also, another thing to keep in mind—if you're wearing white and you make a mess of yourself eating White Trash, nobody will know. You'll just be a little sticky and possibly woozy from all the empty carbs. Folks will just think you're a little drunk, not a pig."

Spread a few feet of aluminum foil, shiny side down, on the counter.

---

continued

Melt 24 ounces white or vanilla bark candy, according to directions in a big bowl (careful—it's easy to burn if you're impatient).

Mix together 2 cups plain Cheerios, 2 cups plain Wheat Chex, 2 cups small pretzel knots, 1 cup almonds (nuts can be raw or toasted but can't have a speck of oil on them), and 1 cup pecans.

Add the dry stuff to the melted stuff and mix gently but thoroughly.

Spread out on the foil to cool.

When cool, you can break up the really big chunks by scrunching them up in the foil.

Heavenly Hash Salad

Quick and easy—just like the kind of girl who has a shotgun wedding. Served religiously by all church groups in Greenville, but the Baptists, who love marshmallows, get the halo.

~~~~

Ingredients
1 can (18¾ ounces) pineapple chunks, drained
2 cups Cool Whip
1 cup shredded coconut
1 cup mini marshmallows
¼ cup maraschino cherries, halved
3 tablespoons milk
3 bananas, sliced
½ cup chopped nuts

Mix all ingredients, gently. Canned fruit is fragile! Let sit overnight in the icebox. This salad can be frozen. Serve on a lettuce leaf—iceberg, of course.

Serves eight.

Holy Roller Salad

So called because it relies heavily on itty-bitty marshmallows, the signature food of the Southern Baptist. Ecumenical note: The Baptists aren't the only ones in town who dote on Holy Roller Salad—we've all been known to enjoy it. But the frugal Baptists are the only ones who also serve it as a dessert.

~~~~

Ingredients
1 can (32 ounces) pineapple chunks, drained
1 cup pineapple juice (saved from above can)
3 cups orange juice
1 cup confectioners' sugar
1/4 teaspoon almond extract
3 apples, diced
3 cans (11 ounces each) mandarin oranges, drained
1 cup mini marshmallows
1/2 cup shredded coconut, fresh or frozen is best
1 cup nuts, pecans preferred but sliced almonds or walnuts will
   work
2 bananas, sliced (optional)

Combine the pineapple juice, orange juice, and confectioners' sugar in a medium saucepan.

Heat until the sugar melts. Cool. Add extract.
Mix the drained fruit, marshmallows, coconut, and nuts.
Pour the cooled juice over fruit. Refrigerate.
Just before serving add the sliced bananas, if desired.

Serves eight.

Faux Champagne

Just right for a shotgun wedding reception—it will perk up
the guests, even if the bride is on the wagon. Because, you
know, you can't drink alcohol if you're PG. However, if it
is being served at a non-shotgun wedding, you might want
to consider having punch "girls" (some not quite fitting
into the *girl* department). When the punch girls were
young, they wore rosebuds or tiny floral tributes (some
wore wrist corsages). They presided over only unspiked
punch. It would not be appropriate for a young girl to pour
anything with alcohol, though they had most likely fetched
a drink or two for their parents at home. The older punch
girls pour the harder stuff and tend to be drawn from the
"always a bridesmaid, never a bride" category. Most likely
she is a cousin of the bride for the day. She wishes she
were pouring martinis for her husband.

Ingredients
¹/₂ cup sugar
1 cup water
1 can (6 ounces) frozen orange juice concentrate
1 can (6 ounces) frozen grapefruit juice concentrate
1 bottle (28 ounces) cold ginger ale
¹/₂ cup grenadine syrup

Bring sugar and water to a boil. Cook for 5 minutes. Remove from heat and when cool add the juice concentrates. Chill in the icebox until it is good and cold. When ready to serve, pour the above mixture in a punch bowl. Add ginger ale and grenadine. Serve at once.

This recipe serves twelve but it is easy to increase.

~~~~

For 250:
12 cups sugar
6 quarts water
12 cans (12 ounces each) frozen orange juice concentrate
12 cans (12 ounces each) frozen grapefruit juice concentrate
24 bottles (28 ounces each) cold ginger ale
4 bottles (25 ounces each) grenadine syrup

Peanut Butter Sticks

Coke (the kind you drink) parties used to be a wonderful way to entertain teenagers and older pre-teenagers—another way of civilizing girls so that they wouldn't grow up to be the kind of girl who has a shotgun wedding. These were casual morning affairs, and there were always elaborate contraptions to hide the bottled Coke. There were little knit stretchy things, coasters, and the like. Some chose to ice their Cokes in the silver punch bowl. The food was much simpler, but always delicious. Those were the good ole days for sure. We'd never heard of Brie en croute.

————

Ingredients
1 loaf Bunny Bread (that would be white)
1 jar (13 ounces) smooth peanut butter
¾ cup vegetable oil

Preheat the oven to 200°.

Remove the crusts from the bread. Toast the crusts at 200° (slow oven) until they are brown and crispy. Allow the crusts to cool and then roll with a rolling pin into fine crumbs.

Cut bread into strips (three or four per slice) and toast in the slow oven until dried out . . . an hour or so, but they must be dried out. Mix peanut butter and oil until blended.

Spread the bread strips or dip them in the peanut butter mixture. Be sure they are coated. Then, roll to coat in the toasted crumbs.

Makes seventy-five pieces (with sticks cut thin).

Saltine Cracker Cookies

To be upscale, use Captain's Wafers instead of saltines.

Ingredients
Saltine crackers
2 sticks unsalted butter
1 cup brown sugar, packed
1 cup finely chopped walnuts or pecans
1 bag (6 ounces) butterscotch chips or Heath English Toffee Bits

Preheat the oven to 400°.

Cover a jelly roll pan with aluminum foil. Place crackers "bumper to bumper" to cover top of pan. In a medium saucepan melt the butter. Stir in the brown sugar. Bring to a boil and cook 2 minutes. Pour over the crackers, making sure each one is coated. Bake at 400° for about 4 minutes. Combine nuts and caramel bits. Sprinkle over the hot crackers.

Put the pan back into the oven until the chips are just melted. Spread evenly. Chill. Peel from foil and break into pieces.

Makes about fifty to sixty pieces.

In a Pickle Black-Eyed Peas

Think of it as caviar, only maybe not beluga. We love our indigenous caviar with cornbread cutouts. Make cornbread thin (bake on a jelly roll pan) and cut with a cookie cutter or into small squares.

~~~~

Ingredients
½ cup vegetable oil
¼ cup red wine vinegar
2 cloves garlic, mashed
1 tablespoon Lea & Perrins Worcestershire sauce
1 bay leaf
1 teaspoon salt
1 teaspoon coarsely ground pepper
½ teaspoon Tabasco
2 cans (16 ounces each) black-eyed peas, well drained
1 yellow onion, thinly sliced

In a saucepan, combine all ingredients except black-eyed peas and onion.

Boil for a minute and pour over the peas and onions. Refrigerate overnight. This is better the second day. Keeps almost indefinitely.

Makes ten.

ORIGINAL ANTS ON A LOG

THE original ants on a log were made with smooth peanut butter and raisins. Simply fill the celery cavity with peanut butter and dot with raisins. We would not suggest this with cocktails!

Ants on a Log

You know it's a child bride when you get this, particularly the version with peanut butter.

Let's start with the best-case scenario.

Ingredients
1 package (8 ounces) cream cheese, softened
1 jar (4 ounces) capers, drained (reserve a few for ants)
1 green onion, thinly sliced
Tabasco
Celery cut into 3- to 4-inch pieces

Mix first 3 ingredients and a splash or two of Tabasco. Chill overnight, if possible, so that the flavors can mingle. Spread the cheese mixture in the celery and put several capers across the top.

Wrong Side of the Track Dip

Honestly, we attended a wedding reception where they had tons of food, and slap-dab in the middle was a silver punch bowl filled with this! We didn't see people turning up their noses, either. We know it's tacky, but we dare you to say it's not delicious.

~~~~

Ingredients

2 cans (10½ ounces each) Fritos bean dip
4 avocados, peeled and cubed
1 lemon
¼ teaspoon salt
½ teaspoon pepper
Tabasco
1 cup sour cream
½ cup mayonnaise
1 package (1.25 ounces) dry taco seasoning mix (McCormick or Lawry's),
1 bunch green onions, chopped tops and all, to equal 1 cup
3 tomatoes, chopped and strained to equal 2 cups
2 cans (3½ ounce each) chopped ripe olives, drained if necessary
8 ounces extra-sharp Cheddar cheese, shredded
Sliced jalapeños, optional

In a 3- to 4-quart bowl: Cover the bottom and up the sides with the bean dip. Mix the avocados with the juice of one lemon, salt, and pepper. Add a few dashes of Tabasco. Spread this over the bean dip. Blend the sour cream, mayonnaise, and taco seasoning. Spread on top of the avocados. Cover with the chopped green onions (use tops and all). Layer with the chopped tomatoes. Top with the chopped olives. Cover the dip with shredded Cheddar.

Top with a few sliced jalapeños (optional).

Lovey-Dovey Breasts

There's no telling how much Wish-Bone dressing Southerners have consumed one way or the other over the years.
If you can't buy or hunt the lovey-dovey doves, you'd
probably better not substitute. Time to start looking for a
Delta hunter to wed?

~~~~

Ingredients
Dove breasts
Wish-Bone Italian dressing
Jalapeño pepper slices
Lawry's lemon pepper seasoning
Tony Chachere's Creole seasoning
Bacon, thinly sliced

Cover the dove breasts with dressing and marinate overnight.
Just before grilling, put a slice of jalapeño between two dove
breasts. Sprinkle with a good shake of lemon pepper and Tony
Chachere's Cajun seasoning.

Wrap a piece of thin bacon around the breast and secure with
a toothpick. Thick bacon will not cook properly, so buy the
cheap stuff.

Grill over charcoal, turning often.

These don't take long. You must watch them, as they will
burn before you know it.

VENISON

WHILE fixin' this, you might want to listen to Junior Walker and the All Stars's classic "Shotgun." It combines shotguns and romance—just like this chapter. Cut across the tenderloin of venison. Cut slices about ½ inch thick. Soak overnight in dressing. Continue to follow the same instructions as for dove.

POULET BANG BANG

IF it moves, shoot it. If it doesn't move, monogram it. And, if it did move and you shot it, stuff it. Southerners love to stuff things. We have passed the point of the stuffed chicken that squirts all over you when you cut it. But the stuffed figs, dates, and apricots remain just as popular. (See recipes on pages 68–69.)

Knock-up Crackers

In England, when you've called somebody on the telephone, you say you've knocked them up. Gayden calls these Knock-Up Crackers because she knocked up Mary Mills Abington for the recipe. Good to offer with drinks. We warn you: These are addictive.

Ingredients
1 envelope Hidden Valley Ranch ranch-style dressing mix
1 cup Wesson oil
1 tablespoon dill weed
1 tablespoon garlic powder with dried parsley
1 box Kroger's oyster crackers
4 dashes Tabasco

Stir the first four ingredients into a mix. Add Tabasco. Then pour in the oyster crackers and cover. Mary Mills uses a Tupperware salad bowl and cover. Turn every 30 minutes or so. When all the mixture is absorbed, put the crackers in Ziploc bags. They will keep for days on end.

Outlaw Chicken

This is a good recipe if you are entertaining your new mother-in-law. The secret is to do everything ahead of time—even if you have to dust your plates before letting your new mother-in-law near the dinner table.

~~~~

Ingredients
10 chicken breasts
One 10¾-ounce can cream of mushroom soup
One 10¾-ounce can cream of chicken soup
1 cup chicken stock
1 medium onion, thinly sliced
1 cup sliced fresh mushrooms (canned only if you must)
¾ cup sliced almonds
¾ cup sauterne

Preheat the oven to 325°.

In a large skillet, brown the chicken in batches. Reserve the drippings.

Arrange chicken in a large oven-to-table casserole.

Using the same browning skillet and drippings, add the 2 soups and the cup of stock. Mix until smooth, and heat. While warming, add the onion, mushrooms, and almonds.

Stir and then add the sauterne.

Cover the chicken with above mixture. Cover tightly.

Bake at 325° for 1 hour. This can be made ahead and reheated. And it's actually better if you do. Serve with rice.

Serves ten generously.

Shotgun Tomatoes with Spinach Filling

Faster than the wedding . . . almost.

> *Six small peeled tomatoes*
> *One box of Stouffer's frozen corn soufflé or spinach soufflé*

Hollow each tomato and drain.
Lightly salt and pepper the inside.
Slighty thaw the frozen Stouffer's.
Fill each tomato with soufflé. Remember they rise.
Bake at 350–375° until golden brown.
Garnish each with a sprig of dill.

6

~~~~

The Mature Bride:
Catching the Last Bouquet

A SINGLE DELTA GIRL, no matter where she wanders, expects to receive a constant stream of wedding clippings from the local newspapers, courtesy of Muh-tha. Mother has not sent these clippings with an eye to sharing another girl's joy. No. A wedding clipping, unless it happens to be your own, is accusatory by nature. One featuring the happy bride-to-be of a spurned suitor is particularly punitive. The only reason Mother does not scribble "See what you let get away, you silly little fool!" is that she doesn't have to.

There is only one thing worse than this gushing river of wedding write-ups: when it stops. When it slows to a trickle and then ceases altogether, there is only one inference possible: You're on the shelf. All the cute girls are married and the supply of eligible bachelors is running as low as Mother's standards have become. The silver and china are destined for the good daughters, the ones who loved Mother enough to get married. Spinsterhood looms. The only way to avert this fate is latching on to the next male with a discernible pulse and joining the ranks of mature brides.

What constitutes a mature bride? Delta girls today are fortunate in having more time to escape this shame than their mothers and grandmothers. Twenty-one was once considered hopeless. If you weren't married by then, you were ashamed to go out in public, which made dating a lot harder. We know a matron, now in her eighties, who skidded dangerously close to her thirtieth year unwed. She was fortunate in her employment—she was the telephone operator. Whenever her reluctant swain attempted to call another love interest, she disconnected him. Unable to make contact with other members of the fair sex, he threw in the towel and married her.

Today there is probably only one group of Delta girls who always get their ring-by-spring: the education majors. There is something about knowing everything there is to know about construction paper and glue that drives the men wild. Other majors may produce degrees, but not the coveted Mrs. degree. Higher education isn't the only impediment to happiness. In the olden days (like a few years before we came along), fathers of daughters spoke of the necessity of having "something to fall back on." It is what today would be called a job. A job would be Precious Baby's last resort if her most promising matrimonial candidate turned out to be a dirty, rotten son of a gun, who left her high and dry. But times—and economic realities—have changed. Delta girls today are encouraged—nay, poked with a cow poke—to enter the job market. Some carry this to extremes, becoming successful executives, who, much to Muh-tha's chagrin, fail to marry at a respectable age. The average age for a first wedding now hovers around twenty-seven—after thirty, the clippings are but a memory. "When sending your children to college," sighs a frustrated mother, "I advise parents to look at the boy-girl ratio. [Pause] We forgot to do this."

Olivia Morgan Gilliam had reached the ripe old age of twenty-four, incipient spinsterhood in her day, by the time of her first marriage. Despite being boy-crazy—she used to talk about SA, which meant sex appeal, but she'd never say anything so vulgar as the s-word—she didn't seem to notice her humiliation. When asked how she had occupied her time between dropping out of All Saints Episcopal High School, where she had elaborately decorated her textbooks with the names of her suitors, and her first special day, Olivia Morgan flashed her what-kind-of-idiot-are-you?-do-you-think-I-went-to-India-to-hep-the-poor? look. "What do you think I did?" she replied somewhat condescendingly. "I went to paw-ties."

Why did we bother to ask? Miss Olivia had such a good time at paw-ties, which were mostly of the dancing sort in her day, that nobody noticed that she was becoming older than the other girls. She eventually fell madly in love with a young man she spotted at a garden paw-tie. The marriage didn't last that long after Herbert got tipsy and stripped nekkid in broad daylight on Main Street.

Before espying Herbert standing by a bed of prize-winning camellias, Olivia Morgan had taught Sunday school at St. James' (where she explained to the children that Jesus was the sort of nice young man who would most certainly have gone to Sewanee, as we call the University of the South, if He'd had the good fortune to be born in the Delta). The children adored her. When they learned that she was engaged, they threw a surprise handkerchief shower, with each child bringing a nice hanky to Sunday school that day. A Southern lady can never have too many fancy handkerchiefs. To the day she died, Olivia Morgan's eyes misted over and she had to dab her eyes with a lace hanky whenever she thought about her handkerchief shower. Thoughts of her husbands produced angrier tears.

Another unmarried belle remained on the dance circuit even longer than Olivia Morgan. Nobody could muster the courage to tell this rapidly aging Isadora Duncan that she was embarrassing herself. Finally, a prominent matron took matters into her own hands. She sent a handwritten note asking the not-so-young thing to serve as a chaperone at the next dance. Chaperones are eagle-eyed older ladies who group themselves around the edges of the ballroom, watching for signs of drunkenness or, worse, faux pas. They are not spring chickens. An invitation to join their ranks was most unwelcome, but the aging belle got the message. Her dancing days ended; her cocktail party days began, proving that there is life after your dancing days are ended. Everybody rejoiced—even in the Delta, where entertainment opportunities are perhaps more limited than in New York City, we eventually tire of watching somebody make a fool of herself.

One Delta family is famous for marrying late. The male

members of the Jeffreys family, which has farmed the same plot of land since Methuselah was a boy, always married late. They were always just in the nick of time to produce a lone heir. When Archer Jeffreys III married—after a comparatively brief courtship of fourteen years—his bride produced not one, but two heirs.

The embarrassed Jeffreys family acted as if she had given birth to a litter. Older brides, of course, mean older bridal attendants. The matron of honor at the Jeffreys wedding (a small affair at St. James', of course, followed by an at-home reception) was visibly with child, her third. When the officiating clergyman asked the wedding party to kneel, he shot a glowering look at the matron of honor. "Not you," he hissed. He was just being careful. The only thing that might have shocked the Jeffreys more than a litter of human children was a matron of honor giving birth during the nuptials.

Unmarried girls past the blush of youth become deeply aware of their plight.

"We're all needier than the United Way," Roberta Shaw, pushing thirty-five, opined as she prepared to leap for Anne Epps Highsmith's bridal bouquet. Precious Billups tripped her and caught it, but Roberta needn't have fretted: Her storied bachelor days were drawing to a close. Roberta was a party girl of wide renown. Dancing on tables at low-down French Quarter bars all hours of the night and day, she'd reiterate her motto, "Eatin's cheatin'," (eatin' is cheatin', because it sobers you up). Some tacky older brides can't resist the allure of a big church wedding with fifty-seven bridesmaids creaking up the aisle. Roberta was not one of these. Having fun until the wee hours doesn't mean you're not a lady. Roberta knew that a small wedding, with the Presbyterian minister performing the rites in the living room, was suitable for a bride in her advanced state of decay. She knew, too, that the invitations should be handwritten. She knew that using a ballpoint pen or anything other than jet-black ink, preferably from a fountain pen, would have made her late mother, the redoubtable Mrs. Robert Shaw, turn in her grave. She knew the correct style of an invitation to the wedding of a mature bride ("Percy and I are to be married at such and such a time, on such and such a date, at such and such a place").

What she did not know was that one person on the guest list, Mrs. Charles Edgar Swain, the most prominent citizen of Alligator, Mississippi, was not a widow. Mr. Charles Edgar Swain was very much alive, though rarely seen in public nowadays. Because of circumstances beyond his control, he was obliged to pass pleasant hours in the attic, with only his dear companion, Mister Jack Daniel's, to help him while away the time. "If you call my house after seven thirty," he used brag, in his freer days, "you're not talking to Charlie Swain—you're talking to Jack Daniel's." (We positively reject the unkind rumor that there was a lock on the attic door.) Having been away from the Delta, Roberta ignorantly addressed the invitation to Mrs. Swain alone. Mrs. Swain may not have entertained the slightest intention of letting Charlie out for a wedding, but she did not look kindly on those who slighted her husband, and—by implication—herself. Her regret arrived by return mail, and Roberta didn't even get so much as a dinky little ashtray from the first family of Alligator.

Spouses seemed to give Roberta particular trouble. While helping her with the invitations, Roberta's friends fell into the bottle. Perhaps this is why one of them inadvertently invited the local clergy without including their wives. (This was back when we had only men of the cloth.) Unlike Mrs. Swain, however, they refused to succumb to false pride. Wild horses can't keep our holy ones away from good food and drink.

Some mature brides are not first-timers. They were not left on the shelf—they got on the wrong shelf. Divorce has always been our dirty little secret in the Mississippi Delta. "When I got my first divorce," bragged Olivia Morgan, a self-described pioneer of divorce, "ladies just weren't getting divorces." Or so we pretended. In truth, more ladies than we cared to admit were getting divorces. Many of us, now in our fifties, sixties, and seventies, grew up with half siblings—and our half brothers and sisters didn't fall from the skies, even though Mama told us that they had. The difference now is that divorce is more open—and more frequent. Some brides and grooms part company by the time their write-up appears in the *Mississippi Magazine* bridal issue. We can't help thinking that, like the tacky groom's cake, this is not necessarily an improvement.

If you marry more than once, the correct wedding order is: First wedding at the church, with all the trimmings; second through third at home; and all subsequent ones at the county courthouse. You might want to go to another county, if the number of weddings is getting really high. Anne Dudley's last wedding—was it four or five?—was joyful but appropriately ill-attended. She chose a courthouse in an undisclosed county. "I certainly couldn't ask anybody to come," averred the always considerate Anne Dudley. "My friends were sick and tired of coming to my weddings."

"We had to be married by a judge, but I didn't care as long as he read the Book of Common Prayer," said another mature bride. In keeping with the dictates of good taste, her wedding—the second for both bride and groom—was held at a friend's house, way out in the country. They recited their vows on the front porch. The host made one big mistake—planting rare azaleas, ordered specially from a florist in another state, in honor of the wedding. They cost an arm and a leg. Even if we could remember for sure who it was, we'd never reveal who was found passed out—we mean napping—in the rare azalea bed the next morning. The bride was nowhere to be found. Her frantic new mate called his new stepson to inquire about her whereabouts. "I reckon she's with you 'cause you married her last night," he replied unhelpfully. A search of the premises turned up the bride: on the sofa in the living room. She, too, was napping. Only one task remained: bailing the wedding guests out of the pokey. The host had supported the wrong candidate for sheriff, and the winner was going out of his way to enforce the drunk-driving laws.

Sad to say, bridegrooms with one foot in the grave are every bit as hard to find as the more sprightly specimens. Old coots as mean as yard dogs get to play the field and date the cutest widows, while women have to pore over the obits to see who's available within courting distance. The Greenville widows are like vultures: When some elderly Adonis loses his wife, the casseroles start pouring into his house. One grumpy old man opened his hand, after shaking hands with a widow, to find she had slipped him a piece of paper with her phone number on it—this was at the funeral parlor.

When Mr. Dick Reeves, who looked like Ichabod Crane, lost his first wife, he became an instant widow heartthrob. Asked to dinner almost nightly, he always showed up with his famous home-baked rolls. The widows oohed and aaahed over his culinary talent. His sister got sick and tired of listening to the widows' raptures. She let slip the truth about Mr. Dick's perfect rolls: "They're Pillsbury," she smugly informed some well-meaning widow. Did this shove Mr. Dick off his pedestal? Not a bit. He had a pulse and could drive. That's about all it takes to set a widow's heart aflutter. The widow set continued to swoon over Mr. Dick's crusty rolls, trying to forget that the only thing crustier was grumpy Mr. Dick.

The thing that took Mr. Dick off the merry-go-round was not coronary failure brought on by hot-buttered Pillsbury rolls. It was his second marriage. It is painful to record that it did not last long. But it was Mr. Dick's own fault: When he drew a map of Greenville for his new bride, a seventy-something newcomer to town, he drew the route to the post office right past the liquor store. When she went to put in her change of address card so her Social Security wouldn't be late, the liquor store was as far as she got. It seems that Mr. Dick's blushing bride liked to tipple. After a speedy divorce, followed by another Pillsbury phase, Mr. Dick at last found true love. This time it was a perfect match: She moved to Greenville, got in the garden club, and gave up all pretense that she gave a big whoop-de-doo about Mr. Dick's silly rolls.

Old Mrs. Bates set her cap for Dr. Henry George, who was a strict, teetotaling Methodist. Mrs. Bates had a sure-proof way of getting him to the altar: seduction. He may have been seduced, but he was still a strict Methodist. Whenever anybody stopped by to see Mrs. Bates after dark, he hid in the hall closet. That way nobody knew they were elderly sinners. "She was cross-eyed and fat, but she had good taste," said a friend of old Mrs. Bates, who was very popular, despite her lack of female pulchritude, and who, by then, was old Mrs. George.

One of our older brides went all the way to Europe to find a groom—but it must have been worth it because she found a handsome one, twenty years her junior. Alice Worthington, an arty divorcée and scion of one of our FFG (First Families of Greenville) families, was traveling in Spain. She had gone to soak up the culture. Not in the first blush of youth, she had a heart attack while walking down the street in Madrid. She collapsed into the arms of a dashing violinist named Jose. He loyally nursed her back to health, returning with her to her native shores, which he loved. Jose wanted to stay in America. Alice consulted the family lawyer. "You have two choices," he told her. "You can adopt him, or you can marry him." It took her about three seconds to make up her mind.

Olivia Morgan did not have to go to Europe or even Sewanee to find her second husband. She found a man closer to home: He was dating her next-door neighbor, Amelie Plunkett, who, like Olivia Morgan, was getting up in years—she was thirty. She had never been married, and this raised Olivia Morgan's sporting instincts. The temptation was irresistible: Why let another girl keep her beau? Olivia Morgan was not above trickery. Every afternoon, at just about the time the gentleman caller, a bald-headed man from Tennessee, was arriving, Olivia Morgan gathered the neighborhood children (including Little Olivia, ten) to play Devil in the Ditch on the front sidewalk. This is a children's game that consists of running back and forth across the sidewalk; it was advantageous in that it allowed a young divorcée to display the gams of which she was so intensely proud, without abandoning the pretense of maidenly modesty. It was a successful maneuver. "Pretty soon I saw the bald-headed man smiling at me," she recalled, remembering yet another triumph over a member of her fair sex. Unfortunately, she got carried away and married him, something she could never quite explain, beyond reporting that he was "very insistent." They married the same weekend her parents had gone to her brother's wedding in Kentucky—she knew that they wouldn't give her permission to marry a total stranger. Making life-changing decisions was not her forte; still, her younger daughter always felt she owed her very existence to Miss Plunkett.

One of the good places to look for an older groom, particularly after the child-bearing years have passed, is in the bosom of your own family. Don't believe it when Yankees sneer at marrying into your own family as something that only happens in Arkansas. Nice people in the Delta are kin to all the other nice people in the Delta, including being kin to themselves. "My grandparents were double first cousins," one of our friends noted, as rude Yankee visitors searched her visage for a twitch or some other telltale sign that what's good for the Hapsburgs might not be as good for the Delta.

One of our most famous mature brides was Mrs. Alcorn Dudley. Mrs. Dudley was a prominent widow whose grandfather had been the governor of Mississippi during our troubles. The Dudleys had more silver than any family in the state being the governor had written to Ulysses Grant a demanding the family silver be returned—it was returned, but the governor's friends were miffed that he addressed Grant "gentleman to gentleman." Mrs. Dudley wasn't looking for a husband, for herself or her daughter, Capitola, who was safely married to an Episcopal clergyman named George Neville. The Nevilles must have been very devout, because George's little brother, Ned, was also studying for the ministry. He was also studying Mrs. Dudley. "I think Ned is infatuated with Mrs. Dudley," Olivia Morgan mused aloud one afternoon as she and her two brothers, also men of the cloth, sat on the front porch in Sewanee. This made the brothers jump up from their chairs and wave their arms in the air. They also ordered her never to say such a thing.

Olivia Morgan didn't have to say it again—it was soon obvious to everybody. Not long after Olivia shocked her brothers, Mrs. Dudley and Ned announced their engagement. Even by Delta standards, it is considered mangling the family tree when a mother becomes her own daughter's junior sister-in-law.

After taking his brother's wife's mother as his lawfully, if highly unusually, wedded wife, Ned did have to confront one serious problem: His bride drove like a bat out of hell. Covering his eyes to avoid the sight of oncoming traffic, he would beg her to slow down—if she was old enough to die, he certainly wasn't! "Oh, hush, Ned," the blushing bride would retort. "I was driving before you were born." Unfortunately, while serving a parish in Alabama, Ned fell head over heels in love with a damsel a few years older than his wife. It was a stuffy era, and Ned was defrocked on account of his divorce.

Another famous mature bride was Weezee Davis of Leland—we have to admit that she was an immature bride, no matter her age. She wasn't a mature bride, even chronologically, the first time she and Sonny Lloyd married each other. Even the second time they wed each other, she wasn't all that ancient, though by the time they tied the knot the third time, she was a mature bride in every way, except for the way she still behaved. Sonny and Weezee had their ups and downs, in every one of their marriages. One down was the time he passed out—or rather took a nap—on the sofa and Weezee was so angry that she came up with the perfect retaliation: She buried his false teeth in the front yard. He never found them. During another of Sonny's alcohol-induced naps, Weezee stripped the recumbent Sonny nekkid, painted his body blue, and arranged him artistically in front of the picture window. A traffic jam on Deer Creek Drive ensued. It must be admitted that Weezee's and Sonny's dress standards slipped with each succeeding marriage; the third time, she wore red tennis shoes, and he wore boll weevil poison. It was crop dusting season. It is a good thing they didn't divorce after that—Mississippi law doesn't allow you to marry the same person more than three times. If the third time hadn't been a charm, they would have had to go to that anything-goes state of Arkansas to get married.

"We never had a cross word," Weezee reminisced after Sonny unexpectedly keeled over dead one day. Some of us had a hard time keeping a straight face. But she was just being smart. Tip to grieving widows on the prowl: Never say that your last marriage was a living hell, even if it was. That is bad advertising. Weezee, by the way, still wears her red tennis shoes, but now she kicks up her heels in Memphis, where she lives happily with her much-younger husband.

As much as we advocate quiet weddings after the first one, some brides just can't control themselves—especially if she happens to be a seventy-something demoiselle engaged to a spry gallant of sixty-three who delights in refilling her whisky glass and lighting her cigarette. Buddy and Eleanor Griffin were such a couple—he's a restoration architect, and Eleanor hoped he'd keep her restored. Like Weezee, Eleanor had married at least one of her husbands more than once. But who's counting? This time it was the real thing. Nothing would do but a wedding at sea in the form of the "wedding package" on a "celebrity cruise," whatever that means. At eighty, Lavinia Highsmith, the senior member of the wedding party (but not by much!), was matron of honor. She was impressed with the ship. "It was the original Love Boat," she boasted. She added, "I'm too old to swim, but I can shop and eat."

The wedding package included the rehearsal dinner, the wedding ceremony, performed by the captain, and a wedding dinner. There was only one thing amiss—thrifty Eleanor refused to buy a new dress. As the mature bride glided up the aisle, given away by a young man who'd left his own young man behind in Houston, it was obvious to all that she had not been on wartime rations since last donning her peach satin wedding frock. "I thought it might split," reminisced the matron of honor. But it didn't. In a moving ceremony, the captain of the ship married them—or we *think* he did; the captain didn't speak word one of English. Mature brides seem to like exotic locales. We know one who planned a scenic wedding at the Grand Canyon. The couple picked up a minister in Las Vegas, the first leg of their journey. As the bridal party descended into the canyon on donkeys, the bride thought to ask the reverend, "What denomination are you, anyway?" "Lady," he replied, "I'll be any one you want me to be."

Before we close, a few words must be said about Anne Dudley's weddings—she could not have been more wrong in saying that we were sick and tired of attending her weddings—at least, we were always willing to attend the receptions. "If only her marriages were as nice as the receptions," said a friend, "everything would have worked out well for Anne Dudley." If anybody knows how to get married, it's the well-practiced Anne Dudley. Her first was a church wedding, followed by a blowout in the backyard on Deer Creek Drive. She received so many wedding presents—we didn't know there would be future opportunities—that a guard was hired to protect them while the wedding party was at the church.

A high-noon wedding—considered the height of elegance in the Delta—was briefly a possibility for Anne Dudley. But few

Delta brides (and especially Anne Dudley) are able to get up this early in the morning, even to get married. The noon wedding therefore remains more of an ideal than something we are actually able to experience. So it was a white-tie affair at eight o'clock. It was the wedding to end all weddings—except that the marriage ended, too. We had such a good time at Anne Dudley's second reception, at her sister's house, that thirteen of us boarded the plane with the bride and groom. Did you have to be a newlywed to want to go to New Orleans?

If anybody has a sense of propriety, it's Anne Dudley—so we were surprised that she chose to marry her third husband in a ceremony at the church. This is against the rule, but maybe it could be justified on the grounds that, as has been noted, Anne Dudley found him at her Bible study class. Perhaps, in addition to Scripture, they bonded over their past marital misadventures— he'd been married and divorced twice, too. During the Communion (not the done thing in the past, but the modern Episcopalian will do anything to add the panache of more ritual—especially the ones who grew up Baptist and are fascinated by ceremony) Anne Dudley plunked herself on the bishop's throne. Somehow this just didn't seem right, though Anne Dudley looked as saintly as if the heavenly hosts were coming to waft her to marital heaven, which was certainly not the case. But the marriage didn't last long, so why carp?

And the reception, like all of Anne Dudley's, was more fun than a barrel of monkeys.

MENU FOR ANNE DUDLEY'S THIRD WEDDING RECEPTION

CANDLELIGHT and white roses were used to decorate for the reception, held at the home of a childhood friend. Candles are an inspired choice for mature guests, because we all look a lot better at our tender ages in the dim flickering of candles.

The cut glass also sparkled. Anne Dudley's own white linens added a nice touch—the hostess was careful not to use any bearing monograms of former husbands! We did use a silver bread basket with a monogram from one of Anne Dudley's previous marriages—but, with a damask napkin lining it, who could tell?

Anne Dudley's sister and brothers sang and played their guitars. Everybody danced. It is no wonder that many say this was Anne Dudley's best wedding reception.

There were three round serving tables. Tables one and two had the same layout: big silver tray, big silver chafing dish. The third table was sweets. At the last minute, we hurriedly arranged kumquats around the wedding cake. Rapunzel, a black and white cocker spaniel, loves chocolate (which isn't good for dogs) and had taken nibbles here and there. The kumquats concealed his depredations nicely.

Black Squid Pasta

Pasta anything was so un-Delta a few years ago, except for spaghetti with red sauce, which is popular at the Delta's Italian restaurants. Now we go to receptions with huge pasta "stations" . . . we guess to feed the hordes.

Pasta bars fit right in with the horrible invention of the sushi bar, martini bar, mojito bar . . . all too often seen at Delta weddings. For a third wedding reception, however, black pasta is fine.

We chose this pasta because it was black—black squid, to be exact and, with the white sauce, it would look beautiful. One pound of pasta will generously serve six as a first course. Of course, served from a chafing dish, it goes a lot further. Cook your pasta al dente and do not rinse. Toss the cooked fettuccini with a bit of cream, at room temperature.

Transfer to the chafing dish and cover with the following sauce.

~~~~

Ingredients
2 cups heavy cream
6 tablespoons butter
2 cloves minced garlic
Salt
White pepper

Nutmeg, freshly grated, i.e., from the nut
1 cup grated Parmesan cheese, the fresher the better, no Kraft's
  (We're not sure the stuff you find in the dried food section is
  even cheese!)

Warm the cream, butter, and garlic over a low flame. Add the salt, pepper, and a few gratings of nutmeg. Simmer for about 10 minutes or until well heated and slightly thickened.

Stir in the Parmesan and toss gently with the pasta.

Garnish with extra Parmesan and a grating of nutmeg.

(If you must go to a kitchen shower—and we pray nobody will give one for a mature bride!—a nutmeg grater and box of whole nutmegs make a nice present. A grating of fresh nutmeg adds another dimension to almost anything . . . particularly brandy milk punch. It also gives the impression that you know what you're doing!)

Serves six.

Mrs. Cheney's Roast

Down here, Mrs. Cheney also means the late Winifred Cheney, one of the best cooks in Mississippi, a Jackson native, and the mother of the Reverend Reynolds Cheney, for years the popular rector of St. James'. Mrs. Cheney's roast was served on the biggest silver tray we could find, with tons of fresh rosemary as a garnish. Of course, rosemary is the herb of remembrance; fondly as we remember the party, we'd like to forget Anne Dudley's third marriage.

This is a marinated roast that must not be overcooked. The original recipe called for a brisket but we have always used a rump roast. Of course, nothing beats a tenderloin, but this is delicious.

~~~~

Ingredients

2 envelopes (0.75 ounce each) dried Good Seasons garlic and herb salad dressing mix

¼ cup apple cider vinegar

1 cup vegetable oil

2 tablespoons water

1 bottle (24 ounces) of ketchup (Use the one that won the race)

14 drops Tabasco

2 tablespoons Worcestershire sauce

Freshly ground pepper

1 pound rump roast, 10 to 12 pounds

Combine the salad dressing mix, vinegar, oil, and water. Stir or shake until blended.

Add the remaining ingredients.

Place the roast in a large roaster or bowl. Pour the marinade over the roast and refrigerate (covered) at least 24 hours. Turn frequently.

Grill outside. Allow the roast to "sit" for 20 minutes before carving.

Slice thinly and serve with homemade rolls.

Serves forty.

THERE WERE THREE CUT GLASS
CONTAINERS HOLDING:

Avocado Mayonnaise

Ingredients
2 cups homemade mayonnaise (see Gayden's mayonnaise, p. 203)
2 green onions, chopped
2 avocados, diced
Lemon juice

Put mayonnaise, green onions, and avocados in a food processor. Process until the avocado is mixed into the mayonnaise. Add lemon juice to taste—about a tablespoon. Chill in an airtight container. If you plan to refrigerate for a while, add the avocado pit to the mayonnaise to prevent it from turning brown, and remove before serving.

Makes two cups.

Gayden's Homemade Mayonnaise

Ingredients
1 large egg
1½ cups vegetable oil
1½ tablespoons apple cider vinegar
1½ teaspoons Tabasco sauce
1 tablespoon lemon juice
½ teaspoon salt
1 teaspoon white pepper

Put the egg in the food processor and pulse for 30 seconds. Add the oil slowly, while pulsing. When the desired consistency is reached, add the other ingredients until they are blended. This doesn't take very long. Taste and adjust seasonings to your liking. If you blend too long, your mayonnaise will be too thick. Refrigerate at least an hour. This will improve the taste.

Makes about two cups.

Horseradish Mayonnaise

Ingredients
½ cup homemade mayonnaise
½ cup sour cream
⅛ cup horseradish (from a jar) or to taste

Combine these ingredients and allow to sit in the refrigerator overnight. Taste and correct the amount of horseradish . . . you might want more!

If using freshly grated horseradish:
2 cups heavy cream, whipped
2 to 3 tablespoons horseradish
Lemon juice

Fold the horseradish into the whipped cream and season to taste with freshly squeezed lemon juice. There is simply no excuse for a bought sauce! This is so easy and delicious.

Makes one cup.

On the second table, we served smoked salmon on a silver tray, with individual compotes containing finely chopped red onions, tiny capers, finely chopped eggs, and whipped and flavored cream cheese. We put the wrapped, seeded lemon wedges in a Revere bowl. Black bread had been cut into heart shapes.

Also on this table were . . .

Charlotte McGee's Chafing Dish Oysters

Hmmm. This reminds me of the old slogan: Eat fish and live longer; eat oysters and love longer. So maybe this isn't the most appropriate choice for a third wedding reception . . . but too late now.

~~~~

Ingredients
1 jar fresh oysters
1 stick unsalted butter
1 teaspoon chervil
1 teaspoon fines herbs

Drain oysters well. They must sit in a colander for a while. It is essential they be free of any extra juice.

Sauté the oysters in the butter. Add the chervil and fines herbs.

Cook the oysters until the edges curl.

This recipe can be doubled.

Makes eight.

Avocado Mousse

We didn't actually serve this, because we had avocado mayonnaise. But this is also delicious served with pickled shrimp. Make this the day before . . . it's better!

~~~~

Ingredients

4 cups chicken broth (use the 32-ounce boxed variety if you do not have homemade, but a well-seasoned homemade broth is much *better)*

4 envelopes unflavored gelatin

4 tablespoons red wine vinegar

6 tablespoons chopped green onions

1/2 cup lemon juice

6 soft avocados, peeled and seeded

1 cup homemade mayonnaise

2 teaspoons Tabasco

2 teaspoons salt

1 teaspoon white pepper

2 teaspoons Lea & Perrins Worcestershire sauce

2 tablespoons minced parsley

2 cups heavy cream, whipped

Using a small saucepan, warm chicken broth over low heat. Sprinkle (do not dump or you will get glue balls) gelatin over the warming broth. Stir until dissolved.

Add vinegar, green onions, and lemon juice. Refrigerate.

In a food processor, process avocados until barely creamed. You want a few pieces of avocado to remain. Do not puree the avocados.

Add the chicken broth mixture, being sure to stir until incorporated.

Add the mayonnaise and seasonings.

Fold in the whipped cream. Taste and adjust seasonings if necessary.

Grease a 12-cup Bundt pan with mayonnaise.

Pour in the mousse mixture and refrigerate overnight.

Makes forty servings for a cocktail party.

THE SWEETS TABLE INCLUDED:

ALMOND DRAGEES

WHEN potpourri first hit the scene, one of our most savvy cateresses put some in a bowl by the wedding book, only to look up and see a male guest putting a big handful in his mouth. Talk about roughage! White candied almonds are traditional at weddings, and they are not only beautiful, but a lot easier to digest! They are also said to be good luck for the guests. We had two compotes, one with white candied almonds, and one with slivered almonds, which are called dragees. For white candied almonds, the number is the Central Grocery in New Orleans: (504)-523-1620. They are also nice as party favors, tied in little silk bags. For silver almond dragees: Diane's in Little Rock, Arkansas. Her number is: (501)-224-2639.

Fried Walnuts

We drove all over the country with fried walnuts (and a nut spoon!) after our first book came out. We briefly lost the nut spoon at the Margaret Mitchell House in Atlanta (if we wanted anybody else to have it, it would be Miss Mitchell's ghost), but it was retrieved for us. The recipe comes from the *Beyond Parsley Cookbook*, which was put out by the Junior League of Kansas City.

~~~~

Ingredients
8 cups water
4 cups English walnut halves
1/2 cup sugar
Cooking oil
Salt

Bring water to a boil, drop in the walnuts, and boil for one minute. Drain the nuts in a colander. Have water running very hot, or use a kettle of boiling water, and rinse.

Drain the nuts well a second time, immediately place them in a bowl, and coat with sugar.

Heat the oil and place the walnuts in the oil about 1 cup at a time, depending on the size of the pan. Fry until golden brown. Remove with a slotted spoon, drain, and place on waxed paper in a single layer. Sprinkle with salt. These can be frozen in an airtight container. Left at room temperature, they remain tasty for a week.

Makes four cups.

7

<em>~~~~</em>

The Wedding Cake: What Do You Do if Your Wedding Cake Weeps?

SOUTHERN MOTHER MIGHT be tempted to marry off her daughter to Jack the Ripper (who reportedly was a member of the royal family—so there) if it meant she could get out all her tea napkins. Many Delta ladies once possessed a special tablecloth called an army navy cloth, which was grand and long enough for the longest tables. The army navy cloth (we don't know why it was called that) was loaned out to adorn the bride's table, where the all-important wedding cake sat, surrounded by garlands of white flowers with perhaps a touch of green ivy. Years before Martha Stewart persuaded the Yankee bride that her wedding cake is "a statement," Delta brides were already making statements. Indeed, the *Mississippi Quarterly* once published a learned article on the significance of the wedding cake in Miss Eudora's *Delta Wedding*. We wonder if literary quarterlies in Massachusetts delve into the metaphysical meaning of the wedding cake. The wedding cake, if you care to delve, was originally a fertility symbol—and the bride's mother is just glad if the cake is cut before there is tangible, rather than symbolic, evidence of fertility.

What we really need in the Delta, of course, is not an erudite treatise on the meaning of the wedding cake but a how-to article on transporting and assembling the cake so that it doesn't make an unintended statement. Since, given the bride's refusal to take sustenance in the months and weeks leading up to the wedding, the cake probably weighs more than she does, this can be complicated. Our mothers still talk about the disaster of the weeping wedding cake. Perhaps it should be known as the incident of the cake that should never have left Memphis. It seems that a prominent family from Como, Mississippi, had spared no expense on ensuring that their eldest daughter—her name was Precious—would have the most memorable cake in the history of the Methodist church of Como—and it turned out to be memorable, all right. The fabulous cake was ordered from Memphis's then-reigning society baker, and Cousin Maudie Lee Poindexter was deputed to fetch it. Unfortunately, the family had neglected to pave Highway 51, then mostly gravel, for the wedding. On about the hundredth swerve to avoid a hound dog, the fabulous cake's top tier fell off and went plop into the lap of the by-then suicidal Maudie Lee. Fortunately, a local baker was called in and he was able to repair the damage, though his gloating proved almost unbearable. His handiwork was short-lived. Precious's beautiful cake began to melt in the Delta heat, or at least the sugar flowers did. Even with air-conditioning (which some of us call air-condition), the life of a Delta wedding cake is short and fraught with peril. The odds for disaster increase exponentially if the cake is the creation of an out-of-town "sugar artist" who has been paid more than the proceeds from last year's crop.

We remember the Atlanta artiste who brought an expensive cake to the Greenville Country Club and assembled it in the ballroom. Then the Leonardo of the sugar flower, unwilling to avail himself of the joys of such local establishments as the Holiday Inn on Highway 82, hopped the next single-engine plane out of town. Almost immediately, a decorative screen fell on the cake. Frantic calls went out to several local bakers, who were otherwise occupied, this being the height of the matrimonial season. The cake was reassembled—sort of—by the bride's hysterical mother and the staff at the country club. Still, several guests commented that this was one wedding at which the cake looked more smashed than the bride's dipso uncle Horace.

Sweetie Pie Sievers, for whom baking was a cross between a hobby and a cottage industry, was for many years one of Greenville's most beloved bakers of wedding cakes. She has, regrettably, taken her recipes to the grave, though Olivia Morgan Gilliam's elder daughter, Little Olivia, cherishes a picture of her wedding cake, a present from Sweetie Pie. There were delicate white sugar trellises, and the cake was topped with pink sweetheart roses grown in Old Mr. Gilliam's garden. Sweetie Pie baked silver charms attached to satin ribbons into the cake. The bridesmaids gathered round to pull out the charms. The one who drew the silver ring would be the next to get married, while the one who got the thimble was supposed to become an old maid (all the bridesmaids were soon married, we are reliably informed). This is a tradition that has fallen by the wayside.

As statements go, we feel Sweetie Pie's genteel wedding cakes were far superior to some of the "unique and one-of-a-kind cakes" proposed by a Mississippi bridal magazine: The article suggests topping wedding cakes with porcelain dolls that look like the couple, "often wearing the same elaborate wedding clothes, embraced with genuine diamond jewelry." We have one word for decadent, jewelry-encrusted dolls atop wedding cakes: no. Sometimes one-of-a-kind is one too many. This is a far cry from the "quaint dolls" an etiquette expert referred to in the 1940s. Wedding cakes are now likely to be square, and white is no longer the rule. We're waiting for the scarlet I-refuse-to-even-pretend-I'm-a-virgin wedding cake.

Mosquitoes, as we have noted, were once upon a time the tiny protectors of a Delta girl's virtue. Unfortunately, these mighty exponents of chastity inevitably exacted a price for their moral vigilance: bites of delicious wedding guests. Now that the virtue thing is no longer an issue, they expect their fleshly homage. To prevent the wedding from turning into such a sacrifice, many families found it essential to spray with DDT. We all grew up loving DDT—it was so much fun to play in the "fog." Look, if you don't get first-run movies, you have to explore other ways to amuse yourself. We chased the DDT truck. Wedding cakes, on the other hand, should not be sprayed with our favorite Delta Chanel. One of our society doyennes scheduled the DDT truck too close to the time of the outdoor reception. Yes, that certain je ne sais quoi was . . . DDT. We regret to report that several guests thought it was the best cake they'd ever put in their mouths. There are now more advanced forms of mosquito repellent, but none have given us as much enjoyment as DDT. So what if we're harboring mutant genes?

The etiquette governing the wedding cake is simple—the bride and groom cut it and feed each other a bite, their first matrimonial act. Couples who feel compelled to smash the cake in each other's faces are to be discouraged. Believe it or not, the wedding cake isn't strictly decorative—the bride cares how it tastes. She most likely has not partaken of sustenance since he popped the question, and is by now almost ready to attack and eat the army navy cloth. The bride isn't the only one who wants a piece of cake—little girls attend weddings for no other reason than the cake. Those little girls who have iron willpower take it home and put it under their pillow for good luck. The bride and groom cut only the first piece of cake and then ladies appointed by the bride's mother, or children—cake girls—do the rest. Because wedding cakes are structured differently from other cakes, the girls have received special instruction in the art of wedding-cake cutting. Some brides still follow the tradition of sending guests home with a piece of cake in a tiny box with a satin ribbon.

We are thrilled when anybody wants to share their hospitality with us, but a wedding is a time when you want to limit your hospitality to the number of people who can be served without resorting to plastic forks. It is better to have a smaller reception, with cake and punch and a few dear friends. We deplore the wedding from hell with an expensive cake, flown in from who knows where, a cast of thousands, and top-of-the-line plastic. There is no such thing as top-of-the-line plastic. We'd rather have church stainless. But, if you've already spent four years of college tuition on one weekend, why not incur the expense of better forks for that fine cake? Think rent-all. They can bring the forks when they deliver the tent.

CYRILLA DUPREL'S SECRET WEDDING CAKE RECIPE

A STALWART of Greenville's "Catholic Carnival," a yearly fund-raiser for the parochial school, Cyrilla Duprel always helped with the cake booth. It featured an array of homemade cakes that you could win by spinning the wheel. She also baked wedding cakes. Most caterers would die before sharing their recipes for wedding cakes. Mrs. Duprel, who has retired to Nashville, graciously shared hers. And what is her super-secret ingredient? Uncle Dunkie's white cake mix. Yes, you got that right, Duncan Hines. Lots and lots of Uncle Dunkie, as the average wedding cake weighs between seventy and a hundred pounds—or just about what the bride weighs if her starvation has paid off—and is five tiers tall. But Mrs. Duprel did develop her own icing.

ICING

Ingredients
1 package (2 pounds) Domino confectioners' sugar, sifted.
1/2 teaspoon each of a combination of orange, pineapple,
  lemon, raspberry, almond, and clear vanilla flavoring
1/2 cup Pet milk or water
1 1/2 cups Crisco shortening

Cream together the liquids (water, flavorings, milk) with powdered sugar. Then add Crisco and beat for at least 15 minutes. Pet milk gives the icing a lovely, ivory color, but for white icing, use plain skim milk or water. Mrs. Duprel always used several batches of this mixture, depending on the size of the cake. Of course, in all likelihood, you will not make your own wedding cake—even if you do know Mrs. Duprel's secrets!

Linda's White Fruit Cake

We are on record as deploring the groom's cake, but if you must have one, this white fruit cake is the best. White fruit cake, not the wedding cake itself, is generally the one put in boxes as wedding souvenirs. This recipe, which appears in *Gourmet of the Delta*, the Bible of Delta cooks, belonged to the late great Linda Haik.

─────

Ingredients
1 pound butter
1 pound sugar
8 or 9 eggs, separated
5 cups flour, sifted before measuring
1 teaspoon baking powder
¼ teaspoon salt
1 teaspoon granulated lemon rind
1 cup candied citron (fruit), slivered
1 cup freshly grated coconut
1 cup white raisins
1 cup candied cherries, whole
1 cup candied pineapple, thinly sliced
1½ cup almonds, blanched
1½ cup pecans

Preheat the oven to 300°.

Cream the butter until it is fluffy and add the sugar slowly, beating well after each addition. "The creaming operation is most important," *Gourmet of the Delta* notes. The yolks should be at room temperature. Add them one at a time, and stir a few times after each addition.

To the balance of fruit and nuts coat with a small amount sifted flour. (Reserve all the cherries and some of the nuts for the last step.)

Combine the remaining flour with baking powder and salt. Stir. Add to the cake mixture.

Stir grated lemon rind into the cake mixture. Then add a portion of the floured nuts and fruit.

After beating the egg whites until they are barely stiff, immediately fold them into the mixture.

Fold in the rest of the fruit and nuts, except for the reserved cherries and nuts.

The cake pan must be lined with greased parchment paper, on the bottom and sides. Pour a thin layer of batter into the pan, and scatter nuts and cherries over this layer. Press lightly on the batter. Repeat.

Add the reserved cherries and nuts to decorate the top during the last hour of baking. Baking time should be about two hours but start checking around ninety minutes.

Betty Carter's Punch

Mrs. Carter was the wife of Hodding Carter, the Pulitzer Prize–winning editor of Greenville's *Delta Democrat Times*. A writer in her own right, Mrs. Carter was a civic leader and all-around force of nature. She made several generations of Greenville tipsy on this potent concoction. This punch was discovered in a treasure trove of Linda Haik's recipes.

This is great punch for a big Delta wedding—as long as you're not a Baptist, and have appointed a designated driver!

~~~~

Ingredients
8¾ cups sugar
16 cups water
Juice of 26 lemons
13 bottles sauterne
9⅘ bottles bourbon
4 bottles brandy
13 bottles club soda
13 bottles grenadine

Boil the sugar and water for 15 minutes and then add lemon juice. Cool. Add sauterne, bourbon, brandy. Before serving, add soda and grenadine.

Makes 600 servings.

Lime Sherbet Wedding Punch

We call punch without alcohol Presbyterian Punch, and we like to have it for teetotalers and children. We all remember lime green punch from going to weddings with our parents. This recipe reminds us of those halcyon days before sherbet became sorbet.

~~~~

Ingredients
1 gallon lime sherbet
4 bottles (28 ounces) very cold ginger ale
1 bottle (28 ounces) club soda
1 can (46 ounces) very cold pineapple juice

In a large punch bowl, combine liquids. Add sherbet and garnish with any or all: orange slices, maraschino cherries, fresh strawberries, sprigs of fresh mint.

Serves at least thirty.

Mrs. Mayhall's Mints

Old-fashioned wedding receptions inevitably included these little mints. Such a nice tradition. Unfortunately, some receptions were color-coordinated: The bridesmaids' dresses matched the punch that matched the mints. Some hostesses got carried away, and before the wedding, they gave bridal Coke parties that featured cream cheese finger sandwiches dyed to match. You haven't lived until you've eaten pink cream cheese on Bunny Bread.

⟋⟋⟋⟋

Ingredients
3 tablespoons butter
5 tablespoons water
1 pound confectioners' sugar
1 teaspoon mint or peppermint extract

Heat butter in water until very hot. Remove from heat and add sugar and extract.

You can add food coloring here, if desired (see above). After the ingredients are well mixed, put them in the tube of an icing decorating set. (I used my cheese straw machine.)

Using the star tip, make small mounds on a piece of foil that has been lightly coated with cornstarch. Allow to rest for 24 hours. The mints will be dry on the outside and be creamy on the inside. They keep well in tins.

Makes seventy.

Mary Lee Hardin's Crystallized Roses

Crystallized roses add an old-fashioned touch. They can be used to decorate a cake or with sugared grapes. Beautiful to look at—sweet to eat. The meringue powder is a specialty item. You will probably need to buy it at a baking shop.

/////

Ingredients

3 tablespoons meringue power
1 16-ounce package powdered sugar, sifted
1 cup water
30 medium to large long-stemmed roses
2 16-ounce packages superfine sugar
48 rose leaves (with stems—you'll need the leaves)

Combine first three ingredients in a large mixing bowl and blend at medium speed with an electric mixer for four to five minutes or until smooth and creamy. Cover tightly and set aside.

Trim stems from one rose three or four inches. Wrap stem in florist tape. (This is optional.)

Spoon ½ meringue mixture into a bowl; cover remaining mixture to prevent drying.

Coat rose petals with meringue mixture. Using a small, soft paintbrush, gently separate large petals from small to make an opening rose. Brush the mixture around tight center bud (do not try to open). Sprinkle roses with superfine sugar, shaking gently to remove excess; dry on a wine rack for at least eight hours (do not cover or chill). Repeat procedure with remaining roses. Crystallized roses may be made up to 48 hours beforehand.

Makes thirty-six.

8

~~~~

The Restorative Cocktail:
We Thought They'd <u>Never</u> Leave.

A S IN OTHER PARTS of the country, the final moment of the public ritual is the couple's getaway. Tradition dictates that the bride must toss her bouquet—regardless of the ensuing carnage—change into a traveling suit (one of the most important ensembles in her trousseau), and depart through a hail of rice or the more ecologically sensitive birdseed. Under the theory that the bride—who is still ravenous, unless she's consumed five or six pieces of wedding cake, which most brides try not to do in public—might not get much farther out of town than the Mickey D's on Highway 82, a picnic basket thoughtfully has been placed among the happy couple's travel effects.

Oddly enough, one of the most popular delicacies in the picnic basket tends to be tiny finger sandwiches with a filling of sliced salmon. Salmon, it should be noted, is a finny friend that isn't grown in our own catfish ponds. When those now slinking toward middle age were growing up, salmon would have evoked one response in a word association game: croquettes. Yes, we thought salmon came from a can. As has been recalled, non-canned salmon may have entered the Delta through Yankee visitors to a wedding reception. It took us a while to get the hang of salmon. At one particularly elegant wedding soiree, Tommy Carnes was seen chewing the plastic sheets between the slices. Though we had figured out by then that salmon had to be sliced, we didn't have enough sense to remove the divider sheets—or maybe a drunk front had moved in and we didn't care.

A historically more Delta-appropriate filling is Virginia ham, thinly sliced and on a beaten biscuit (more on beaten biscuits in a second). Since Delta people think of themselves as FFVs—that stands for First Families of Virginia—who, by an accident of birth, weren't born in Virginia, Virginia ham is one of our favorite things. It reminds us of our old Virginia homes that we've yet to see. Old Mr. Gilliam's constant—and we do mean constant—boast was that he really had been born in the Commonwealth. Every year, he made a trip to his native land, returning with Virginia hams to hang in his back hall. Proud non-cook that she was, Olivia Morgan Gilliam succumbed and went into the kitchen to prepare the beaten biscuits required. She used to say that Mr. Gilliam stood over her with a whip, but that was not true. He would never whip a daw-tah. He merely paced, looking as if he were experiencing the onset of adult starvation. When Mr. Gilliam died, and Olivia Morgan moved out of her father's house (a move, incidentally, not accomplished during either of her two marriages!), one of the things she took was the beaten biscuit brake. She didn't intend to make beaten biscuits again (or, indeed, anything the nice people at Stouffer's hadn't baked and pre-frozen for her), but a beaten biscuit brake is almost as dear to a Southerner as the family silver. A heavy marble table (marble keeps the dough cool) with rolling pins and ornate iron legs, it is about the size of a sewing machine table. You have to run the dough through the rolling pins several hundred times. A brake also feels like it might weigh several hundred pounds. The men from the moving van company referred to Olivia Morgan's beloved brake as a "hernia table." She cautioned them against such vulgar language. She also put a potted plant on the brake, to celebrate her liberation.

Unfortunately, getting the bride to the point that she is ready to drive off into the gloaming with her new husband and thinly sliced ham is no small feat. The convivial spirit of the Delta bride is such that it has been known to militate against a timely departure. One of our more lively brides held her reception at the Peabody Hotel in Memphis. Her frantic mother had coaxed her from the dance floor and onto the elevator, and they were going upstairs so the bride could change into her travel suit. The MOB was flooded with relief. But it was premature. When the elevator door opened, there stood a rowdy assemblage of young men, celebrating Ole Miss's latest football victory. It was just too much for a loyal Chi Omega! Hoisted onto the shoulders of the revelers, the bride headed off down the street. Above the din, she could be heard shouting, "Forward, Rebels, march to fame. Hit that line and win this game." The MOB knew that, if her daughter didn't return fairly soon, she would definitely march into the matrimony hall of fame.

Not many brides—even Chi Os—choose to spend their wedding night with Rebels fans, other than the one they are marrying. The hysterical MOB was contemplating calling the police, when the bride suddenly returned. But the trial was not over. Somebody had packed only half the bride's travel suit—the lower half. By this time, the bride didn't much care. Half naked? Try half looped. She was so looped, in fact, that she started singing the Arkansas fight song. The MOB made a quick decision that her daughter would break with protocol and depart in her by now not-so-white wedding gown. We hope she didn't have to wear it all the way to Bora-Bora, the honeymoon destination. (Whatever happened to Niagara Falls?)

When Olivia Morgan Gilliam made her famously spur-of-the-moment second leap into holy matrimony, her gallant took her for their first night of wedded bliss to the Leland Hotel. Old Mr. Gilliam was beside himself with anger that his daw-tah, whom he adored, had been fool enough to marry somebody who took her to a hotel not twelve miles from Greenville to celebrate their alliance. Moreover, for the wed or the unwed, the Leland Hotel, though hardly a fleabag, was a poor substitute for the Peabody. Old Mr. Gilliam was still fulminating about the ignominy of the Leland Hotel long after the marriage was consigned to the dust of divorce court dockets.

Although the groom pays for the wedding trip, the bride's parents care almost as much about the destination as do the principals. They hope it will reflect both generosity and financial stability on the part of their daughter's new husband. It must also impress the other mothers at the Thursday morning gatherings at the Hair Tenders. But this is not the only concern.

Southern mothers don't want their daughters to go to the powder room—where the poor dears might forget to put tissues on the toilette seat!—alone, much less on a honeymoon with a strange man. If not prevented, the bride's mother will attempt to chaperone the happy couple. A local travel agent told us about the poor soul who slinked into her office and, with a hangdog air, admitted that his first honeymoon had not been a success. The problem was the presence of his new mother-in-law. The mother-in-law had kindly offered her vacation house—without bothering to inform them that she came with it. Perhaps not surprisingly, this marriage was not a roaring success. *This time* the groom-to-be was taking no chances. He begged for some out-of-the-way destination to which flights had to be booked months, if not years, in advance.

Many couples, exhausted from partying at their reception, secretly spend the night in town and leave for their wedding trip the next morning. Sometimes, however, this is tricky. When it comes to accommodations, we are not the Riviera. One couple stayed in the nicest motel in town—that's also where Uncle Jim Bob and Aunt Billie from Nitta Yuma stayed the night. We are told that making small talk at the breakfast buffet was awkward. That isn't the most uncomfortable fancy-meeting-you-here story we've heard. One Delta businessman had the misfortune of marrying on the same day as his ex-girlfriend—her engagement picture had appeared in the newspaper, opposite his fiancée's, the same Sunday. Adding insult to injury, both couples arrived at the breakfast bar at the same hotel in Jackson at the very same moment. It is our understanding that our friend didn't invite the other couple to sit with him and his blushing bride.

At least they hadn't stayed all night at his reception, as all too many couples seem in danger of doing nowadays. It used to be that even the most famous round heels (so known because rounded heels let you *rolllll* over . . . backwards) feigned sufficient innocence on their wedding nights to pretend something new was in store and leave the reception at a decent hour. This was good for all of us because newlyweds—like royal personages—generally are the first to leave the reception. It would be heartless of close friends not to wait to bid them farewell. Nowadays, parents must forget to instill this rubric, and we find ourselves ready to shove the happy couple out the door. One bride stayed so long, we thought we were going to have to beat her with a stick. Her poor mother was so exhausted that she passed out. All the guests were hanging on, trying to remain sentient—or at least standing—while waiting for the bride and groom to leave. Finally the bride, perhaps sensing that something was amiss, asked a doyenne, "When can we go? Everyone is still here."

"We thought they'd never leave," said a bitter aunt as she hurled her birdseed with a vengeance. These girls just want to par-tee. We've heard it a million times: "I have all my friends here and this is a wonderful party, great food, music; why should I leave?" So the guesties can go home, for one reason (and to show you're a blushing bride, even if this calls forth your best thespian skills). But like so much else, maybe this last vestige of nice manners will go, too.

Some couples, fortunately, have an inbred gentility that tells them that it just isn't nice to spend your entire wedding night cavorting with hundreds of your nearest and dearest. Theoretically, you should be cavorting with your new husband. Even if you are having more fun than a barrel of monkeys, you should pretend that you're going off to cavort with your new spouse. Roberta Shaw and her new husband could have partied all night, as, indeed, the couple and all their friends had done in nightly revels that preceded their at-home nuptials. But Roberta is a lady. She and her new husband tore themselves away from the festivities at a decent hour, spending their wedding night clandestinely at a friend's house. The next morning, they got up bright and early to fly to Eureka Springs, a beautiful Victorian town nestled in the Ozarks.

Of course, after days and nights of manic celebration, they felt like death warmed over. They were set to uphold another fine old Delta tradition: hair of the dog that bit you. That's what we in the Delta call a toddy for the body that has already had quite a few toddies. Of all the hangover remedies that don't actually work, we regard this one as the best. Roberta and her beloved rang for room service and prepared to feel human again. It was then that they discovered a horrible truth: Eureka Springs was a dry county. Being a dry county in Mississippi never meant that you couldn't drink like a fish. Everybody visited the bootlegger frequently. But in some places dry meant dry; the neon lights outside the window of Roberta and her beloved, flashing temperance messages, did not help their throbbing headaches. But the marriage has lasted, and that's what matters.

As the couple departs, if they depart, the MOB, who has for the last six months been, in effect, running a business, still has an important obligation to fulfill: She must ruin the initial months of the marriage by relentlessly hounding the bride about ... thank-you notes. Southerners are obsessed with thank-you notes. Why, goes a joke, don't Delta girls engage in group sex? Because they'd have to write too many thank-you notes. There are Southerners who will write you a diabetes-inducing thank-you note if you so much as nod at them across the back alley. "Thank you for nodding at me. It was a truly beautiful moment that I will always cherish." Southern families view the writing of thank-you notes as a competitive activity. Mothers expect their children to have X-ray vision so they can write their Christmas notes before actually opening the gift. Mothers mentally chalk up the time it takes nieces and nephews to do their notes, and, if their own children are beaten in this all-important race, they will suffer intensely—but not in silence. "There's not an important event in my life that wasn't wrecked by Mama's harping on thank-you notes," says Jane Bell Dixon.

A bride has a year to write thank-you notes for her wedding gifts. She must use nice quality informals. Traditionally, these informals were the first time she used her new name. Maybe today it's the first time she uses her new hyphenated name. Since a note from a Southern girl must be personal, with a telling anecdote, thank-you notes require a certain amount of art. In small Southern towns, there are ladies whose claim to fame is that they write nice notes. It has been said that a note from a well-bred Southern girl, who has been taught to gush, gush, gush from day one, never has a fill-in-the-blank feel. That is why it was so shocking that one of the most august ladies in the Delta sent . . . fill-in-the-blank thank-you notes. She had been to one of the finest finishing schools in the country, and it was said that on cold days, she often mused, "Why aren't the other girls wearing their furs?" She had fill-in-the-blank cards that duplicated her own handwriting. Nobody would ever have guessed that they were fill-in-the-blank cards, if Aunt Amelia hadn't accidentally mailed them before the bride had . . . filled in the blanks. An old lady from Leland still recalls the shock of receiving a thank-you note from such a lovely bride informing her, "Horace and I will certainly enjoy using your thoughtful BLANK."

It was the single most shocking event in Delta marital history until Annie Wade took a shotgun to her husband, George. He did not survive, but she had a good lawyer. Strangely, over lunch at the Leland Café, Annie Wade recently confided to an elderly friend, "I sure do miss George." "Then why did you kill him?" the older lady asked. We were so afraid Annie Wade would take it the wrong way. But she was a lady and so she pretended she hadn't heard.

Just to prevent having to shoot yourself because you can't get your notes written fast enough to satisfy your mother, some brides send out an engraved card saying the gift has been received and a thank-you note will follow. This gives you ample time to dream up sweet personal anecdotes to flatter some old coot you hope you never have to lay eyes on again. It also lets the sender know that the gift has arrived—and that it's just your ill-bred rudeness, not the postal service, that's responsible for their delay in receiving the note.

After the family has helped pick up the egg rolls behind the ficus trees at the Greenville Country Club—rest assured that whatever was served at the wedding will be on the menu for Sunday lunch—and returned the borrowed silver, and done some intermediate harassing about notes, the MOB and her husband are entitled to another Delta tradition—the restorative cocktail. The poor MOB and FOB have been called upon to exercise amazing restraint . . . starting right off with the groom. It's time they have the opportunity to "let it out and let go" . . . that's really what the restorative cocktail is all about. They may be headed for the poorhouse, but that should not stop them from getting out the best liquor—not the Old Mr. Boston that might have been served at the reception!—and relaxing with their friends.

A restorative cocktail, with only your good friends—and not all the people you've had to include at the wedding—is a good use for wedding leftovers, and a time to celebrate—and to cross your fingers for the two young (or not so young) people who have just been launched. We wish them all the happiness—and good luck—in the world. Here's to them—and to us, for surviving their wedding festivities!

Beaten Biscuits

Make these on the day that you don't feel like weeding or pruning. It's very therapeutic to abuse something that is going to turn out delicious. You have to be tough with this dough. Whether you use a beaten biscuit brake or an axe handle, you must beat the dough until it blisters. Also, make sure your biscuits are tiny. Southerners like small, small and thin, thin, thin. Small biscuits and thin ham, that is. We know that's extra nice. Gentlemen learn to carve at an early age . . . something they learn from their fathers and grandfathers. Some are so good that it makes the local surgeon blush.

〜〜〜〜

Ingredients
1½ teaspoon salt
Pinch of sugar (optional)
4 cups flour
1 cup shortening
1 cup very cold milk
Extra flour for preparing the biscuit brake

Preheat the oven to 400°.

Sift salt, sugar, and 4 cups of flour together. Cut the shortening in using two silver knives.

Add the milk slowly until a stiff dough is formed. Beat the

dough with a heavy rolling pin and fold. Beat and fold. Turn, beat, and fold. Continue for about 15 minutes or until the dough is silky smooth and small blisters appear (on the dough, not on your fingers). The dough should also be very shiny.

Roll to a thickness of about an inch or less. Cut to the size of a quarter and prick the tops with the tines of a fork. Bake at 400° on an ungreased baking sheet for 15 minutes or until the top is creamy in color . . . not brown or even close. You should have a multilayered delicacy that is served with the thinnest possible sliver of ham.

If you are using a biscuit brake:

Flour the brake and the rollers. Work the dough through the rollers for at least 15 minutes, or until the dough is shiny and blistered. Roll to an inch or less in thickness. Cut and prick. Bake according to the above instructions.

Makes forty to fifty.

Fig Loaf and Lime Cream

These are lovely and delicious, appropriate for the bridal picnic basket or as a pickup food for the restorative cocktail.

~~~~

Ingredients
1 stick unsalted butter
1 cup sugar
3 eggs
2 cups all-purpose flour
1½ teaspoon cinnamon
1 teaspoon baking soda
1 teaspoon salt
1 cup milk mixed with 1 teaspoon white vinegar
32 fresh figs, or enough to make two cups, pulverized

Preheat the oven to 350°. Cream the butter and sugar. Add eggs one at a time. Mix flour, cinnamon, soda, and salt. Add by the quarter cup to the creamed mixture. Add milk and vinegar mixture. Using a food processor, pulse the figs until just pulverized. Do not over-process. Fold 2 cups of processed figs into the batter, making sure that the figs are evenly distributed. Fill a large greased loaf pan (12 × 4¾ works nicely). Smooth the top. Bake at 350° for approximately 1 hour or until firm to the touch.

Allow the loaf to cool slightly and turn out. Cool completely before slicing.

DELICIOUS FINGER SANDWICHES

Slice the loaf and then use a decorative (fluted) biscuit cutter to make small rounds. Cover each round with lime cream and follow with a piece of shaved ham or prosciutto. Slick ham just will not work.

LIME CREAM

1 lime
1 cup sour cream

Squeeze the juice from half the lime into the sour cream. Taste and add the juice from the other half if necessary. If you like a strong lime flavor, use the entire lime.

Makes forty.

Linda's Shrimp Custard Tarts

This is an old recipe of Linda Haik's. While these little tarts could be served at the reception, they are also ideal for a restorative cocktail party. If prepared for the reception, be sure to use small individual tart pans.

~~~~

Ingredients
1 pound shrimp, peeled and deveined
4 slices bacon
1/2 cup grated Parmesan cheese
4 eggs
2 cups milk
2 teaspoons thyme
3 teaspoons Tabasco
Salt and pepper

Preheat the oven to 450°.

Line tart pans with pre-made pastry. Arrange the shrimp on the bottom of each pan. Cook the bacon until crisp, and then crumble and sprinkle over the shrimp. Sprinkle a layer of Parmesan cheese over the bacon. Beat eggs slightly. Add milk, thyme, Tabasco, salt, and pepper. Pour into pastry shells. Bake at 450° for about 20 minutes. Don't overbake, because that will dry the tarts.

Serves eight.

MARINATED TOMATOES AND
AVOCADOS

WHEN Linda Haik served marinated tomatoes and avocados, everyone wished for a spoon (a big one). Seems it was particularly aggravating when there were no forks or plates . . . just skewers. Linda had hundreds of gallon glass jars that she would always use to marinate this. She would travel to the party with these jars filled and then drain and serve. There was never any left. Linda always served this in a wide, shallow glass bowl. She left behind no recipe, but her imitators do it this way:

Peel and slice six tomatoes, then quarter each slice. To peel a tomato, dip it quickly in boiling water; that will make it easy to slip the knife right in under the skin. Peel and thickly slice six avocados. Cut into "chunks." Peel and thinly slice two yellow onions. In a glass jar, layer the above ingredients, starting with the onions. Cover with your favorite vinaigrette. Chill. Drain well before serving. Depending on your vinaigrette, you could use a dash of salt and a generous grind of fresh black pepper.

Vinaigrette

Olive oil is just like whisky: Buy the best you can afford. We always try to pick some up good olive oil when we're in Memphis. Linda's vinaigrette may be lost to posterity, but this one goes well with her legendary tomatoes and avocados.

~~~~

Ingredients
½ cup olive oil
½ cup vegetable oil
⅓ cup vinegar, or a bit more to taste
3 cloves garlic, minced
1 teaspoon whole-grain Dijon mustard
1 teaspoon salt
2 teaspoons coarsely ground black pepper
Pinch of sugar (optional)

Place all ingredients in a jar and shake until blended. Chill.

JANE HOVAS'S TURKEY HASH

FOR the day of the wedding brunch, serve this hash on halved cornbread squares, slathered with butter. It's a wonderful dish to have on hand because it will keep well for the exhausted family and pesky guests to eat in the days following the main event. The late Mary Adleine McKamy, another great cook, who was good at putting menus together, helped Jane develop this recipe. She always suggested a peach half filled with chutney and sprinkled with sherry to accompany this. Jane Hovas is one of the best cooks in Greenville, and we felt we owed the world the benefit of Jane's culinary genius!

Jane gave this to us in steps:

1. Bake a 14-pound Butterball turkey, de-bone, and save fat.
2. Cook 2 packages chicken breasts and 2 packages thighs and legs in celery, onion, carrots, and peppercorn. De-bone and save and strain the broth.
3. Brown 2 cups flour in an iron skillet in 250° oven.
4. Sauté the following in turkey fat: 4 chopped onions, 1 chopped bell pepper, 1 chopped celery stalk. When done, lift out with slotted spoon

continued

and add to chopped, de-boned turkey and chicken.

5. Add browned flour to turkey fat and make a roux. Use chicken broth to thin. Add to turkey mixture.

6. Sauté 2 pounds sliced mushrooms in 1 stick butter. Add 1 pound grated carrots. Cook until done and add to turkey and chicken meat.

7. Adjust seasonings (salt, pepper, kitchen bouquet, Lea & Perrins Worcestershire sauce).

8. Add more chicken broth until the mixture reaches the desired consistency. Serve over cornbread squares.

Makes twenty to thirty servings.

Ann Shackelford's Watermelon Pickle

This recipe came from Ann's paternal grandmother, Irma Alston Jennings, from Clarksdale, Mississippi. It was her trademark recipe. Passed down by her aunt Medora Sifford Jennings, it came in handwritten form to Ann's mother, Dot Jennings of Little Rock. When Ann's aunt and grandmother teamed up to make this, Mrs. Jennings would turn away so Aunt Medora wouldn't see how much oil of clove she was using. Mrs. Jennings took this secret to her grave, and so the amounts are approximate. This is an excellent accompaniment to restorative cocktails.

⁓⁓⁓⁓

Ingredients
15 pounds watermelon rind, cut into 1-inch squares, all pink and green removed
1 cup lime
2 tablespoons alum (an old-fashioned canning agent)
Sugar
1 quart cider vinegar
1 quart water
1 teaspoon oil of clove
1 teaspoon cinnamon
3 pieces ginger root
3 lemons, sliced thin

Cover rind with water and add lime. Soak overnight. Next morning, wash thoroughly. Cover with water again. Add alum and bring to a boil. Boil for 45 minutes. Wash thoroughly again, and soak in ice water for 1 hour (this keeps it crisp, and you don't want it to go mushy). Mix sugar, cup for cup, with rind, cider vinegar, water, oil of clove, cinnamon, ginger root, and lemons. Boil until rind is tender—a toothpick should go through it easily. Put in sterilized jars, cover with boiling water, and seal.

Makes at least eight pints.

Dot Jennings's Red Caviar Molds

This is a savory treat that is an excellent accompaniment for cocktails. Using larger molds, you can also make it as a salad. A heart-shaped red caviar salad would be nice at a bridal luncheon.

~~~~

Ingredients
1 tablespoon unflavored gelatin
¼ cup cold water
1 cup boiling water
1 grated onion
½ teaspoon salt
½ teaspoon white pepper
½ cup heavy cream
½ cup mayonnaise
Juice of ½ lemon
1 large jar red caviar
Salad oil for greasing

Dissolve gelatin in water. Add 1 cup boiling water, grated onion, salt, and white pepper. Stir until dissolved. Then put in the refrigerator until it begins to thicken. Beat cream and mix with mayonnaise (preferably homemade) and lemon juice. Add gelatin and gently fold in red caviar. Fill decorative molds greased with salad oil. Refrigerate until set. Should unmold easily when inverted. May be served with dressing.

~~~~

Dressing:
¾ cup mayonnaise
Chopped chives and parsley
2 tablespoons lemon juice
1 teaspoon A.1. sauce
2 tablespoons ketchup
Salt and pepper to taste
Small amount of cream

Mix and thin with a little cream.

Makes eight as a first course.

All the Rage Tomato Bites

Tacky—but men love tacky. Pass these with drinks.

~~~~~

Ingredients
1 cup shredded Swiss cheese
½ cup mayonnaise
½ tablespoon grated onion
1 can diced Rotel tomatoes, well drained
1 teaspoon dried basil
8 slices bacon, fried and chopped

Preheat the oven to 400°.
Combine the above and fill miniature phyllo or pastry cups.
Bake at 400° for 10 minutes.

Makes thirty servings.

Todd Lane's Oyster Roll

An old-time hit. This recipe has been popular year in and year out.

~~~~

Ingredients
3 tablespoons mayonnaise
2 packages (8 ounces each) cream cheese
2 teaspoons Lea & Perrins Worcestershire sauce
Garlic to taste
2 cans smoked oysters, chopped
Parsley

Cream mayonnaise into cheese to hold it together. Add Worcestershire sauce.

Combine.

Spread about ½ inch thick on waxed paper. Add garlic to oysters and spread them on top of cheese mixture.

Roll as for a jelly roll.

Chill 24 hours.

Cover with parsley before serving. Serve with crackers (not saltines).

Serves twenty.

Acknowledgments

We are blessed with wonderful friends. Our old friends encouraged us, gave us parties, recipes, and stories. Perhaps most significantly, they did wring our necks for delving into their family stories in the first book (and again in this one—we're counting on more foregiveness). Suffice it to say: Nothing in life is more golden than friends, especially old friends, and most especially those who are the possessors of a sense of humor, that most humanizing quality. We'd have to cut down a forest to name all the Southern friends and relatives who've made this book both possible and so much fun. So we'll simply say: You know who you are. Thanks Roberta, Ann Dudley, and all the gang.

We've been lucky in our Yankee friends too. It's safe to say that this book would not have come to fruition without Gayle Ross, our agent, who had faith in the project and the ability and convey that faith to Hyperion. We thank Bob Miller, Will Schwalbe, and Ellen Archer for taking a chance on us. Leslie Wells, our astute and sensitive editor, would probably have been just as smart if she weren't from Virginia. But we loved it that she is and felt that she could make suggestions from a depth of knowledge. Stella Connell is a New York publicist who hails from Mississippi—and we're glad she was on our team too. Stella is athe gold standard for moving books off the shelves and into the reader's hands.

We will always be grateful to Susan Mercandetti and Jonathan Burnham for getting the ball rolling with the first book and to Sandra McElwaine just happening to mention to Susan that she knew "these crazy Southern friends" who had a book idea.

Index

Index

Index